Let the Word dwell in you.

With *Explore the Bible*, groups can expect to engage Scripture in its proper context and be better prepared to live it out in their own context. These book-by-book studies will help participants—

> › grow in their love for Scripture;

> › gain new knowledge about what the Bible teaches;

> › develop biblical disciplines;

> › internalize the Word in a way that transforms their lives.

Connect

@ExploreTheBible

facebook.com/ExploreTheBible

lifeway.com/ExploreTheBible

ministrygrid.com/web/ExploreTheBible

ISBN 978-1-4300-4510-4
Item 005756888

Dewey decimal classification: 222.43
Subject headings: BIBLE. O.T. 1 SAMUEL / BIBLE. O.T.—HISTORY OF BIBLICAL EVENTS / PROPHETS

ERIC GEIGER
Vice President, LifeWay Resources

MICHAEL KELLY
Director, Groups Ministry

ERIC GEIGER
General Editor

JEREMY MAXFIELD
Content Editor

Send questions/comments to: Content Editor, *Explore the Bible: Small-Group Study;* One LifeWay Plaza; Nashville, TN 37234-0152.

Printed in the United States of America

For ordering or inquiries visit *www.lifeway.com;* write to LifeWay Small Groups; One LifeWay Plaza; Nashville, TN 37234-0152; or call toll free 800.458.2772.

Session 1 quotation: Martin Luther, as quoted in E. M. Bounds, *Purpose in Prayer* [online, cited 14 January 2016]. Available from the Internet: *www.ccel.org.* Session 2 quotation: Charles Spurgeon, as quoted in Ernest W. Bacon, *Spurgeon: Heir of the Puritans* (Arlington Heights, IL: Christian Liberty Press, 1967), 115. Session 3 quotation: C. S. Lewis, *The Weight of Glory* (New York: HarperCollins, 2001), 26. Session 4 quotation: J. R. R. Tolkien, *The Lord of the Rings,* vol. 1, *The Fellowship of the Ring* (Boston: Houghton Mifflin Harcourt, 1966). Session 5 quotation: Mark Twain, *BrainyQuote* [online, cited 25 January 2016]. Available from the Internet: *www.brainyquote.com.* Session 6 quotation: Jackie Robinson, as quoted in Mark Newman, "1947: A Time for Change," *MLB News* [online], 13 April 2007 [cited 14 January 2016]. Available from the Internet: *http://m.mlb.com/news/article/1895445/.*

❯ ABOUT THIS STUDY

The Bible is an amazing gift from our awesome God. In it He reveals Himself and His glory for us to witness. I'm excited that you're joining this journey through the Book of 1 Samuel. It's truly epic and beautiful in its scope and message.

In 1 Samuel we see the story of God's people. As we do, we see the greatness of our God over His people. He's worthy. He's holy. He's the God above all gods, the King above all kings. As your group discusses this book, I want to encourage you to see the overarching theme of God's greatness as the umbrella that encompasses each story.

So many times life takes its toll on us, and we're prone to take our eyes off God and His great sufficiency for us. Therefore, your discussions and emphasis on God's greatness and the victories He wins for His people will be a great reminder and encouragement. In 1 Samuel God's greatness will be a constant background as you discuss stories of deliverance, victory, forgiveness, and worship.

As you study the passages in their context and seek to obey them in your context, I know the Lord will encourage you and challenge you. Enjoy the journey through 1 Samuel. Our God is still great, still cares for His people, and is still the King above all kings.

The **Explore the Bible** series will help you know and apply the encouraging and empowering truth of God's Word. Each session is organized in the following way.

UNDERSTAND THE CONTEXT: This page explains the original context of each passage and begins relating the primary themes to your life today.

EXPLORE THE TEXT: These pages walk you through Scripture, providing helpful commentary and encouraging thoughtful interaction with God through His Word.

OBEY THE TEXT: This page helps you apply the truths you've explored. It's not enough to know what the Bible says. God's Word has the power to change your life.

LEADER GUIDE: This final section provides optional discussion starters and suggested questions to help anyone lead a group in reviewing each section of the personal study.

For helps on how to use *Explore the Bible*, tips on how to better lead groups, or additional ideas for leading, visit: **www.ministrygrid.com/web/ExploreTheBible.**

❯GROUP COMMITMENT

As you begin this study, it's important that everyone agrees to key group values. Clearly establishing the purpose of your time together will foster healthy expectations and help ease any uncertainties. The goal is to ensure that everyone has a positive experience leading to spiritual growth and true community. Initial each value as you discuss the following with your group.

❑ PRIORITY

Life is busy, but we value this time with one another and with God's Word. We choose to make being together a priority.

❑ PARTICIPATION

We're a group. Everyone is encouraged to participate. No one dominates.

❑ RESPECT

Everyone is given the right to his or her own opinions. All questions are encouraged and respected.

❑ TRUST

Each person humbly seeks truth through time in prayer and in the Bible. We trust God as the loving authority in our lives.

❑ CONFIDENTIALITY

Anything said in our meetings is never repeated outside the group without the permission of everyone involved. This commitment is vital in creating an environment of trust and openness.

❑ SUPPORT

Everyone can count on anyone in this group. Permission is given to call on one another at any time, especially in times of crisis. The group provides care for every member.

❑ ACCOUNTABILITY

We agree to let the members of our group hold us accountable to commitments we make in the loving ways we decide on. Questions are always welcome. Unsolicited advice, however, isn't permitted.

_____   _____

I agree to all the commitments.   Date

❯ GENERAL EDITOR

 **Eric Geiger** serves as the vice president of the Resources Division at LifeWay Christian Resources. Eric received his doctorate in leadership and church ministry from the Southern Baptist Theological Seminary. He has authored and coauthored several books, including *Creature of the Word* and the best-selling church-leadership book *Simple Church*.

Eric also serves as the senior pastor of ClearView Baptist Church in Franklin, Tennessee. Eric is married to Kaye, and they have two daughters, Eden and Evie.

› CONTENTS

ANSWERED

God answers the prayers of those who humbly seek Him.

> ABOUT 1 SAMUEL

AUTHOR

The human writer of 1 Samuel isn't mentioned in Scripture, though it bears the name of the prophet who was the bridge between the time of the judges and the beginning of the monarchy in Israel. Although Jewish tradition attributes the book to Samuel himself, this is unlikely because the events described extended past the life of the prophet. First Chronicles 29:29-30, however, mentions a historical collection that appears to have been written by Samuel, so it's safe to assume that the writer of 1 Samuel used this resource and possibly the writings of the prophets Nathan and Gad.

DATE

Two questions emerge in any discussion about the chronology of 1 Samuel. First, at what time did the events in the book occur? It's fairly certain that they took place from 1105 to 1010 B.C.

Second, when were the events of 1 Samuel actually written in the historical narrative we know today? Most conservative scholars believe the book was written sometime either during King Solomon's reign (around 950 B.C.) or perhaps after the kingdom divided in 931 B.C. The reference to the kings of Judah in 1 Samuel 27:6 could possibly indicate the latter date.

PURPOSE

First and Second Samuel were originally one document in the Hebrew Bible. This fact no doubt informs any attempt to understand the writer's purpose. Both books provide accounts of the emergence of kingship and the history of the kingdom of God in Israel. The narrative is built around three major characters: Samuel, Saul, and David.

A study of 1 Samuel will reveal the primacy of God's glory. While the lives of some characters (Samuel and David) reflected His greatness and goodness, others (Eli, his sons, and Saul) made a mockery of God and defamed Him by their actions. These lessons will lead us to confront the call to exalt God alone.

> "I HAVE SO MUCH TO DO THAT I SHALL SPEND THE FIRST THREE HOURS IN PRAYER."
> —Martin Luther

❯ 1 SAMUEL 1:10-18,26-28

Think About It

Note all of Hannah's self-descriptors in this Bible passage.

How did she define herself in relation to Eli the priest?

In verses 10-16 identify the emotions Hannah experienced.

10 Deeply hurt, Hannah prayed to the Lord and wept with many tears. **11** Making a vow, she pleaded, "Lord of Hosts, if You will take notice of Your servant's affliction, remember and not forget me, and give Your servant a son, I will give him to the Lord all the days of his life, and his hair will never be cut." **12** While she continued praying in the Lord's presence, Eli watched her lips. **13** Hannah was praying silently, and though her lips were moving, her voice could not be heard. Eli thought she was drunk **14** and scolded her, "How long are you going to be drunk? Get rid of your wine!" **15** "No, my lord," Hannah replied. "I am a woman with a broken heart. I haven't had any wine or beer; I've been pouring out my heart before the Lord. **16** Don't think of me as a wicked woman; I've been praying from the depth of my anguish and resentment." **17** Eli responded, "Go in peace, and may the God of Israel grant the petition you've requested from Him." **18** "May your servant find favor with you," she replied. Then Hannah went on her way; she ate and no longer looked despondent.

26 "Please, my lord," she said, "as sure as you live, my lord, I am the woman who stood here beside you praying to the Lord. **27** I prayed for this boy, and since the Lord gave me what I asked Him for, **28** I now give the boy to the Lord. For as long as he lives, he is given to the Lord." Then he bowed in worship to the Lord there.

> UNDERSTAND THE CONTEXT

USE THE FOLLOWING PAGES TO PREPARE FOR YOUR GROUP TIME.

Change was in the air during the time of the events recorded in 1 Samuel. The priesthood had grown corrupt. Neither Eli nor his sons, Hophni and Phinehas, served the Lord in a way that honored Him. God, therefore, would bring an end to Eli's priestly dynasty (see 1 Sam. 2:12-36). It also was a time of transition in government from a theocracy (the rule of God) to a monarchy (the rule of a king). Samuel, the child born through God's intervention, would be a stabilizing force during these days of upheaval and transition. Samuel would anoint the first two kings of Israel but to different outcomes. The first king, Saul, proved unfit for the office. Therefore, God would call out the young shepherd David to lead His people.

It would be a mistake to assume that everything in Israel rose and fell because of the people in positions of power. In the opening chapter of the book, we meet an ordinary woman in great distress who prayed to God. Hannah played a key role in the unfolding of God's plan and purpose for Israel. She was one of two wives of Elkanah, a man of the tribe of Ephraim, and she was unable to have a child. This is a traumatic situation in any era or culture but especially so in ancient Israel, where children were viewed as evidence of God's blessing and favor. Hannah prayed for a child, and God heard and answered her. The child born to Hannah was Samuel. In gratitude Hannah gave the child back to the Lord because she loved the Giver more than the gift. Her prayer in 1 Samuel 2:1-10 is a triumphant celebration of the power of God to overturn human designs and anticipates the emergence of kings in Israel (see v. 10).

› EXPLORE THE TEXT

HANNAH'S PRAYER (1 Samuel 1:10-11)

¹⁰Deeply hurt, Hannah prayed to the LORD and wept with many tears. ¹¹Making a vow, she pleaded, "LORD of Hosts, if You will take notice of Your servant's affliction, remember and not forget me, and give Your servant a son, I will give him to the LORD all the days of his life, and his hair will never be cut."

As a part of their normal practice, Hannah and her husband, Elkanah, went to Shiloh, the place of worship in Israel, to offer a sacrifice to the Lord. With the taunts of her rival, Peninnah (Elkanah's other wife), about her barrenness ringing in her ears (see vv. 6-7), Hannah went to the Lord's tabernacle, where Eli the priest was serving. A literal description of the state of Hannah's heart in verse 10 is "bitter of soul." The phrase is repeated in 22:2 to describe those who, because of desperation in their lives, rallied around David as king. The purest prayer comes from desperate devotion and a believing heart that can find relief and help only from God. In His compassion the Father takes notice of all our grief and sorrow.

Why is it important to be honest with God about our pains and frustrations?

As Hannah prayed, she made a vow to the Lord. This raises the question of whether it's advisable to promise God to do a certain thing in response to His answering a prayer. Our relationship with God is based on grace. We can't earn His favor or benefits. In Hannah we see the heart attitude to which God favorably responds. In the original language she called herself a servant or slave to the Lord. A deep understanding of the Lord's greatness and of our position in relation to Him drives and motivates prayer. Thus, prayer isn't a means to secure what we want for ourselves but rather a submission of everything in our lives to His control.

In asking the Lord to remember her, Hannah wasn't seeking to jog the memory of God. Rather, she was asking Him to act in her behalf. In return, Hannah's promise to God was that her son would be a lifelong Nazirite (see Num. 6:1-7). Unlike the Levitical priests, who served from age 25 to 50 (see 8:23-26), this boy would forever be in the service of the Lord.

What role does submission play in prayer? How are humility and submission to God related?

ELI'S AFFIRMATION (1 Samuel 1:12-18)

¹²**While she continued praying in the LORD's presence, Eli watched her lips. ¹³Hannah was praying silently, and though her lips were moving, her voice could not be heard. Eli thought she was drunk ¹⁴and scolded her, "How long are you going to be drunk? Get rid of your wine!"**

Though Eli was likely past the age of service for serving as a priest, he was monitoring activity in the tabernacle (see v. 9). As he observed Hannah's praying, he mistook fervency in whispered prayer as something irreverent and concluded that she was intoxicated. Perhaps the type of praying demonstrated by Hannah was uncharacteristic of that time, and Eli wasn't accustomed to seeing prayer practiced that way. Eli accused Hannah of being drunk and scolded her to sober up. Perhaps he'd witnessed such abuses in the tabernacle in the past, but he completely misread this woman. He could watch her lips, but he couldn't see into her heart.

¹⁵**"No, my lord," Hannah replied. "I am a woman with a broken heart. I haven't had any wine or beer; I've been pouring out my heart before the Lord. ¹⁶Don't think of me as a wicked woman; I've been praying from the depth of my anguish and resentment."**

KEY DOCTRINE
Stewardship

Christians should recognize their time, talents, and material possessions as entrusted to them to use for the glory of God and for helping others.

Hannah replied to this rebuke with humility. She was even willing to subject herself to a priest whose discernment could be questioned. Perhaps the greatest test of our servanthood comes in our relationships with others. Serving the Lord is one thing, but being willing to humble ourselves before other people is something else.

¹⁷Eli responded, "Go in peace, and may the God of Israel grant the petition you've requested from Him." ¹⁸"May your servant find favor with you," she replied. Then Hannah went on her way; she ate and no longer looked despondent.

Eli realized that he had misread Hannah. He blessed and encouraged her with a priestly benediction after recognizing God was at work in that moment. The point isn't that our prayers should impress others to the point that we receive validation from them. We should pray sincerely and trust that God will affirm our petitions, whether through human encouragement or inner confirmation by the Holy Spirit based on His Word.

Hannah's response to Eli again revealed her humility. The word translated *favor* (see v. 18) also can mean *grace* (KJV) and describes undeserved favor. With respect to God, grace is His unmerited favor that He extends to sinners when they repent and believe in His Son, Jesus Christ (see Eph. 2:8-9).

Notice the difference in Hannah's attitude and demeanor as she left the place of prayer. Though her circumstances hadn't changed, after prayer she was transformed. Prayer does that for us as well. When we get up off our knees, confident that God has heard us and will act according to His will, we can reengage life with a new attitude.

On what basis can we know that God has heard our prayer? What promises can we claim from Scripture?

HANNAH'S PRESENTATION
(1 Samuel 1:26-28)

²⁶"Please, my lord," she said, "as sure as you live, my lord, I am the woman who stood here beside you praying to the LORD."

BIBLE SKILL
Compare passages with related themes.

Compare 1 Samuel 2:1-10 and Luke 1:46-55.

At what points are the two songs similar?

How are they different?

What conclusions can be drawn about God from these two songs?

After her encounter with Eli in the tabernacle, Hannah went home to Ramah with her husband. God answered her prayer, and she bore a son whom she named Samuel, which meant *name of God.* His name indicated the divine intervention that came through his mother's prayer (see vv. 19-20). After Samuel was weaned (usually around age 3), Hannah took the child to the annual sacrifice to dedicate Samuel to the Lord permanently (see vv. 21-22). Elkanah had the prerogative under the law to overrule her vow (see Num. 30:10-15), but he did not do so. Instead, Elkanah affirmed her plan, no doubt indicating his own devotion to the Lord (see 1 Sam. 1:23). Hannah reminded Eli of their previous encounter in which she prayed to the Lord while standing beside him, lost in communion with God.

²⁷"I prayed for this boy, and since the LORD gave me what I asked Him for, ²⁸I now give the boy to the LORD. For as long as he lives, he is given to the LORD." Then he bowed in worship to the LORD there.

God gave Hannah a child, and she gave the child back to God. Though she would later bear other children with God's help (see 2:21), Samuel would remain at the tabernacle in service to the Lord. Only those who know the Lord through meaningful prayer attain to the deepest commitments.

How does seeing an answered prayer encourage the person who prayed? How does it encourage others who were aware of the prayer?

❯ OBEY THE TEXT

We can approach God with our frustrations and heartfelt desires, knowing we can trust Him to do what's best. We encourage others by praying with them in agreement, sympathizing with their heartaches. God is praised when we recognize that all we have and are come from Him.

Describe your greatest disappointment in life at this moment. Take time to pray about this issue, following the example set by Hannah.

Discuss with the group how prayer with others can be a source of encouragement. Identify actions the group can take this week to encourage one another through prayer. Record prayer needs and put into practice the actions identified.

List ways God has answered your prayers in the past. With whom can you share this list as an act of worship and thanksgiving to God?

MEMORIZE ❯

"Hannah prayed: My heart rejoices in the LORD; my horn is lifted up by the LORD. My mouth boasts over my enemies, because I rejoice in Your salvation."
1 Samuel 2:1

USE THE SPACE PROVIDED TO MAKE OBSERVATIONS AND RECORD PRAYER
REQUESTS DURING THE GROUP EXPERIENCE FOR THIS SESSION.

MY THOUGHTS

Record insights and questions from the group experience.

_____

_____

_____

_____

_____

_____

MY RESPONSE

Note specific ways you'll put into practice the truth explored this week.

_____

_____

_____

_____

_____

_____

MY PRAYERS

List specific prayer needs and answers to remember this week.

_____

_____

_____

_____

_____

_____

KING

Only God is worthy of being acknowledged as the Ruler of His people and of His creation.

UNDERSTAND THE CONTEXT

The Book of 1 Samuel is greatly focused on the issue of kingship. Two of the three main characters, Saul and David, were kings. The third main character, Samuel, instituted the monarchy and anointed these initial regents. In the Hebrew ordering of the books of the Old Testament, 1 and 2 Samuel follow Judges and precede 1 and 2 Kings. In this way, they serve as a transition between the old era of the judges and the new era of the kings.

Provision for kingship had been made during the time of Moses (see Deut. 17:14-20), though it was never God's perfect intention. Sometimes in dealing with His people, God granted a sinful request but not without painful consequences (see Ps. 106:15). Because a monarchy would eventually play a role in the coming of Jesus, the Messiah (see Luke 1:32-33), the desire for a king by the people actually fell under the scope of God's permissive will.

One aspect of God's dealings with His people was His testing of their commitment to obey His commands through various circumstances (see Judg. 3:1-4). The leaders of Israel, whose desires evidently mirrored those of the people as a whole, sought a king because of their fears about impending threats from other nations (see 1 Sam. 9:16; 12:12). In this way, they departed from the ways of their forefathers who followed Moses at the Red Sea and allowed the Lord to fight the battle with the Egyptians for them (see Ex. 14:13-14). The threats on the horizon from the Philistines and the Ammonites served as tests of the Israelites' faithfulness to God.

"GOD HAS SET APART HIS PEOPLE FROM BEFORE THE FOUNDATION OF THE WORLD TO BE HIS CHOSEN AND PECULIAR INHERITANCE."

—Charles Spurgeon

→ 1 SAMUEL 8:4-9,19-22

Think About It

In these passages highlight the reasons the people of Israel gave for seeking a human king.

What are the flaws in each excuse?

4 All the elders of Israel gathered together and went to Samuel at Ramah. **5** They said to him, "Look, you are old, and your sons do not follow your example. Therefore, appoint a king to judge us the same as all the other nations have." **6** When they said, "Give us a king to judge us," Samuel considered their demand sinful, so he prayed to the LORD. **7** But the LORD told him, "Listen to the people and everything they say to you. They have not rejected you; they have rejected Me as their king. **8** They are doing the same thing to you that they have done to Me, since the day I brought them out of Egypt until this day, abandoning Me and worshiping other gods. **9** Listen to them, but you must solemnly warn them and tell them about the rights of the king who will rule over them."

19 The people refused to listen to Samuel. "No!" they said. "We must have a king over us. **20** Then we'll be like all the other nations: our king will judge us, go out before us, and fight our battles." **21** Samuel listened to all the people's words and then repeated them to the LORD. **22** "Listen to them," the LORD told Samuel. "Appoint a king for them." Then Samuel told the men of Israel, "Each of you, go back to your city."

❯ EXPLORE THE TEXT

A KING DEMANDED (1 Samuel 8:4-5)

⁴All the elders of Israel gathered together and went to Samuel at Ramah.

Samuel's home was in Ramah (see 7:17), a town associated with the tribe of Benjamin. After conferring, all the elders of Israel came to Ramah to talk to Samuel. This meeting would have monumental consequences for the nation. There's no mention that the gathered leaders intentionally searched for the Lord's will prior to approaching Samuel. If the Lord is truly the ruler of His people, then seeking His will should be the primary focus.

⁵They said to him, "Look, you are old, and your sons do not follow your example. Therefore, appoint a king to judge us the same as all the other nations have."

The basis for the elders' approach of Samuel was his advancing age and the dereliction of duty by his sons. Samuel's sons didn't walk in his ways and practiced self-serving leadership (see 8:1-3). Although some Bible students question Samuel's appointment of his sons as judges, he may have done so from both practical considerations and obedience to the law. They served in Beer-sheba, located some distance away in the southern part of the nation. As Samuel aged, travel may have become more difficult for him. He needed assistance in discharging his duties. God's plan has always involved multiple leaders (see Deut. 16:18-20). The problem was that Samuel's sons didn't live up to God's standard for leaders.

The elders, who represented the thoughts and desires of the people as a whole, drew an erroneous conclusion from the deficient leadership of Joel and Abijah, the sons of Samuel. They likely feared what might happen after Samuel died and his sons assumed leadership. Although this may have been a legitimate concern, the elders' conclusion possibly revealed a lack of faith in God on their part.

What about their request for a king? Was that a sinful request? After all, didn't Moses make provision for a king in the law (see Deut. 17:14-20)? The key to understanding this dilemma is found in the words of the elders: "the same as all the other nations have" (1 Sam. 8:5). Their request wasn't an attempt to deepen their obedience to the law, thereby fulfilling their covenant responsibilities to God. Rather, it was an inordinate desire to be like the other nations around them.

In their request the elders were admitting something about themselves. They wanted to be like the other nations in spite of the fact that the Israelites were called to be distinct and different. Exodus 19:5-6 says they were to be God's "own possession out of all the peoples" of the world, a "holy nation." In Leviticus 20:26 God said He had set them apart from all the rest of the nations to be His own people. Yet they weren't interested in being that. In asking for a king over them, the elders were revealing that they wanted to be like all the other nations. In so doing, they were actually rejecting God's rule over them by seeking a human king. Sometimes we can put so much faith in another person that we completely dishonor God.

How does a desire to be like other people affect a person's values and character? How does that desire cloud a person's decision making?

REJECTION DECLARED (1 Samuel 8:6-9)

⁶When they said, "Give us a king to judge us," Samuel considered their demand sinful, so he prayed to the LORD.

The literal rendering of Samuel's response to the request is strong: "The thing was evil in the eyes of Samuel." However, true to the nature of a biblical prophet, Samuel didn't rely on his own estimation but took the matter to the Lord. Samuel prayed, and in doing so, he set an example for every believer. By taking the situation into the presence of the Lord, the prophet was able to rise above mere personal resentment over the request.

7But the LORD told him, "Listen to the people and everything they say to you. They have not rejected you; they have rejected Me as their king."

God had appointed and called Samuel to lead the people as His representative. To reject the Lord's messenger and prophet was to reject the Lord Himself. Therefore, it's surprising to read that the Lord then told Samuel to grant the people's wish instead of rebuking them for their disobedience. Sometimes the greatest act of judgment on God's part is to simply give people what they seek. Conversely, when God says no to His children, it can be one of the most gracious things He does for them.

8"They are doing the same thing to you that they have done to Me, since the day I brought them out of Egypt until this day, abandoning Me and worshiping other gods." 9"Listen to them, but you must solemnly warn them and tell them about the rights of the king who will rule over them."

God told Samuel that the people's response to him was akin to their disloyalty to the Lord. Samuel had aged, and the people thought he was either no longer sufficient for the task of leadership or no longer relevant for the times. They were wrong on both counts. God's ability to lead and provide for them hadn't diminished at all.

While Samuel was instructed to give the people what they wanted, the Lord also instructed him to warn them about the dangers of an earthly king. While they were crying out for a king, God knew someday they'd cry out because of a king (see v. 18). In verses 10-17 Samuel used the word *take* six times to describe the way coming kings would rule the people. While the people's focus was on what they'd receive by having a king, God painted a picture for them of what they'd lose. One danger for any human ruler is the sinful tendency to exploit one's position for personal gain. As our Shepherd, Christ contrasted Himself with a thief who comes to take, not give (see John 10:10-13).

KEY DOCTRINE
God

God is the Creator, Redeemer, Preserver, and Ruler of the universe.

BIBLE SKILL

Synthesize multiple passages related to a similar theme.

Review the following passages, identifying guidelines for ways Christians should relate to their government or ways they should govern:

Matthew 20:20-28

Romans 13:1-7

1 Peter 2:13-19

Record the insights you gained about government and governing.

What does a believer lose by relying on a human authority more than Christ? How can we determine when we should rely on a human entity and when we shouldn't?

REBELLION DETERMINED
(1 Samuel 8:19-22)

¹⁹**The people refused to listen to Samuel. "No!" they said. "We must have a king over us. ²⁰Then we'll be like all the other nations: our king will judge us, go out before us, and fight our battles."**

Samuel's warning didn't deter the people; their hearts were set on having a human ruler. The level of intensity in their quest increased. The selection of a king moved from being preferred to becoming a necessity: "We must have a king over us" (v. 19). Their true inclinations were exposed in their admission that they would become like all the other nations. Originally, they'd simply asked for a king as all other nations had. In response to prophetic warnings, their true spiritual colors emerged.

What do the descriptions of the desired king in verse 20 reveal about the people's hearts?

Specifically, the people wanted a king to do two things: judge them and fight their battles. They were abdicating their responsibilities as citizens in God's community while simultaneously seeking to dislodge the Lord God from His role as Israel's champion in battle (see Deut. 20:4; Judg. 4:14). In their eyes the battle was no longer the Lord's but theirs. Such is typical of human beings. Sometimes we seek to be less than what God calls us to be, and on other occasions we overreach and try to replace the true God.

Eventually, Israel would be given a king who would recognize that the battle belonged to the Lord (see 1 Sam. 17:47). David would become a model for what a true human king of Israel should be. Even in the face of the defiance of His people, God was still merciful and would eventually bring forth good from the evil in the hearts of His people.

²¹Samuel listened to all the people's words and then repeated them to the LORD. ²²"Listen to them," the LORD told Samuel. "Appoint a king for them." Then Samuel told the men of Israel, "Each of you, go back to your city."

In contrast to his earlier prayer, Samuel simply repeated the words of the people to the Lord. When disbelief prevails, chaos sets in. While the people should have listened to their prophet, the Lord instead instructed Samuel to obey the voice of the people. Such turbulence is the inevitable result of a failure to see God alone as the Ruler and King. Likewise, when people today fail to acknowledge Jesus as the King of kings and Lord of lords (see Rev. 19:16), personal chaos will be the inevitable result.

What does God's allowing Israel to have a king teach us about God?

Some people speculate about why Samuel sent the people home instead of immediately initiating the process of finding a king. There's no need to imagine that Samuel was trying to delay the inauguration of a king. However, his behavior contrasted with that of the people. The selection of a king would need the guidance and direction of the Lord, and as the Lord's messenger, Samuel would wait on God for counsel. Confessing God as Ruler is one thing, but it's something else to trust Him enough to wait on His guidance.

OBEY THE TEXT

God desires His people to be distinct from others, trusting Him in all matters. When we reject God's leaders and their warnings, we reject God. We can trust God to provide godly leaders even when we're tempted to take matters into our own hands.

Identify fears or anxieties that threaten your trust in the Lord's guidance and provision. What can your group do to strengthen each person's faith?

Evaluate your life, looking for times when you rejected God's leaders or the messages they presented. What actions do you need to take to respond to these godly leaders' warnings and leadership?

Who are the leaders God has placed in your life who give you godly counsel and direction? Record a prayer, thanking God for them and asking God to give them courage and direction to lead you well.

MEMORIZE

"The LORD told him, 'Listen to the people and everything they say to you. They have not rejected you; they have rejected Me as their king.'" 1 Samuel 8:7

USE THE SPACE PROVIDED TO MAKE OBSERVATIONS AND RECORD PRAYER
REQUESTS DURING THE GROUP EXPERIENCE FOR THIS SESSION.

MY THOUGHTS

Record insights and questions from the group experience.

_____

_____

_____

_____

_____

MY RESPONSE

Note specific ways you'll put into practice the truth explored this week.

_____

_____

_____

_____

_____

MY PRAYERS

List specific prayer needs and answers to remember this week.

_____

_____

_____

_____

_____

JUDGED

Judgment awaits those who reject God's instruction.

❯ UNDERSTAND THE CONTEXT

Even prior to his enthronement as king, disturbing signs existed about Saul's lack of regard for the Lord's commandments. Saul's initial appearance in Scripture indicated little interest in or awareness of divine revelation. He didn't know where the prophet Samuel could be found (see 1 Sam. 9:6,18). Samuel was revered in every area of the kingdom (see 3:20), but Saul seemed to be out of the loop in regard to the ministry of Israel's judge and prophet. Also, Saul seemed to think the favor of a prophet could be purchased (see 9:7-8).

Early in his reign Saul disregarded God's direct instruction. Partial obedience is still disobedience, and this would become a trend in the spiritual trajectory of Saul's life. Although he followed Samuel's instruction to go to Gilgal (see 10:8), he disregarded the prophet's schedule for the offering of sacrifice. In direct violation of Samuel's command, Saul offered the sacrifice of burnt offering himself. When challenged about this by the prophet, Saul blamed his soldiers, Samuel, and the Philistines (see 13:11-12). Saul claimed to seek the Lord's favor (see v. 12), but God's blessing doesn't come through disobedience.

One of the major themes of 1 Samuel is the honor of God (see 2:30). The priest Eli dishonored God by his failure to correct his sons, who desecrated the sacrifices offered to God by consuming them for themselves (see vv. 12-17,27-29). Saul also dishonored God by his disobedience and in the end suffered greatly as a result.

"WE ARE HALF-HEARTED CREATURES ... FAR TOO EASILY PLEASED."

—C. S. Lewis

Think About It

*Notice the different
ways Saul's actions are
described or defined
in these passages.*

*Compare and contrast
the descriptions by
considering who is
describing the action.*

*Outline the steps
Samuel took after
God informed him
of Saul's actions.*

7 Saul struck down the Amalekites from Havilah all the way to Shur, which is next to Egypt. **8** He captured Agag king of Amalek alive, but he completely destroyed all the rest of the people with the sword. **9** Saul and the troops spared Agag, and the best of the sheep, cattle, and choice animals, as well as the young rams and the best of everything else. They were not willing to destroy them, but they did destroy all the worthless and unwanted things. **10** Then the word of the LORD came to Samuel, **11** "I regret that I made Saul king, for he has turned away from following Me and has not carried out My instructions." So Samuel became angry and cried out to the LORD all night. **12** Early in the morning Samuel got up to confront Saul, but it was reported to Samuel, "Saul went to Carmel where he set up a monument for himself. Then he turned around and went down to Gilgal." **13** When Samuel came to him, Saul said, "May the LORD bless you. I have carried out the LORD's instructions." **14** Samuel replied, "Then what is this sound of sheep and cattle I hear?" **15** Saul answered, "The troops brought them from the Amalekites and spared the best sheep and cattle in order to offer a sacrifice to the Lord your God, but the rest we destroyed."

22 Then Samuel said:

> Does the LORD take pleasure in burnt
>   offerings and sacrifices
> as much as in obeying the LORD?
> Look: to obey is better than sacrifice,
> to pay attention is better than the fat of rams.
> **23** For rebellion is like the sin of divination,
> and defiance is like wickedness and idolatry.
> Because you have rejected the word of the LORD,
> He has rejected you as king.

❯ EXPLORE THE TEXT

SAUL'S DISOBEDIENCE *(1 Samuel 15:7-9)*

⁷Saul struck down the Amalekites from Havilah all the way to Shur, which is next to Egypt. ⁸He captured Agag king of Amalek alive, but he completely destroyed all the rest of the people with the sword. ⁹Saul and the troops spared Agag, and the best of the sheep, cattle, and choice animals, as well as the young rams and the best of everything else. They were not willing to destroy them, but they did destroy all the worthless and unwanted things.

God gave a command to Saul that he was to kill every living person among the Amalekites, and he was to slaughter all their livestock (see v. 3). This policy, often called the ban, was rarely given in the Old Testament. It was a directive that no one could be spared and that no plunder could be taken after a conquest. This was God's righteous judgment on an entire nation for its sinfulness and the fulfillment of a sentence pronounced years earlier (see Deut. 25:17-19). Saul partially obeyed the command God gave him. He completely destroyed all the people except for their king, Agag. By taking Agag alive, Saul disobeyed the Lord.

The text mentions for the second time that Saul disobeyed the Lord's command in regard to King Agag. Notice that he spared Agag when God specifically told him not to spare anyone (see v. 3). The text doesn't tell us the rationale, only that Saul didn't do what God instructed him to do. Perhaps it's good to be reminded that there's no good reason for disobeying God.

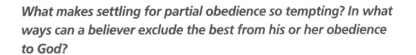

What makes settling for partial obedience so tempting? In what ways can a believer exclude the best from his or her obedience to God?

The Amalekites, whose leader Saul spared, were ancient enemies of God's people. They'd attempted to thwart the Lord's redemptive purposes for Israel. God's command to completely destroy Amalek was recompense for past transgressions. Saul, on the other hand, had no sense of history, only a sense of what he wanted in the moment.

SAMUEL'S CONFRONTATION
(1 Samuel 15:10-15)

¹⁰Then the word of the LORD came to Samuel, ¹¹"I regret that I made Saul king, for he has turned away from following Me and has not carried out My instructions." So Samuel became angry and cried out to the LORD all night.

As He had done many times in the past, God spoke to Samuel. Years ago the prophet had demonstrated his suitability to hear from God because of his yielded heart and his willingness to do whatever He asked (see 3:10-17). Saul demonstrated no such suitability by his chronic impatience and disobedience. In this he failed to follow the Lord God. The hallmark of a great king, like David, was that he completely followed Yahweh, the God of Israel (see 1 Kings 11:6). Saul's behavior brought sorrow to God's heart and righteous indignation to Samuel's heart. Samuel spent the whole night in anguished prayer. Perhaps he pleaded with God to give Saul another chance. But it wasn't to be.

¹²Early in the morning Samuel got up to confront Saul, but it was reported to Samuel, "Saul went to Carmel where he set up a monument for himself. Then he turned around and went down to Gilgal."

After God told him what the king had done, Samuel got up to confront Saul. We may think our disobedience goes unnoticed, but that isn't the case. We may come to the place of accepting our sin, but a holy

God doesn't. Samuel was told that Saul went to build a monument for himself. While Saul was seeking honor for himself, God's honor had been diminished through disobedience. Ultimately, all sin is a blight on the honor of God, and all judgment is the restoration of His glory.

What makes confronting someone about his or her disobedience a challenge? What risks are involved in confronting someone? What risks are involved when we don't confront someone?

KEY DOCTRINE
God

To God we owe the highest love, reverence, and obedience.

¹³**When Samuel came to him, Saul said, "May the LORD bless you. I have carried out the LORD's instructions." ¹⁴Samuel replied, "Then what is this sound of sheep and cattle I hear?" ¹⁵Saul answered, "The troops brought them from the Amalekites and spared the best sheep and cattle in order to offer a sacrifice to the LORD your God, but the rest we destroyed."**

Samuel tracked Saul to Gilgal for a decisive confrontation. As he had previously done (see 13:10), Saul greeted the prophet as if nothing at all was wrong. He seemed to have no remorse over his action. And then he claimed that he'd carried out the Lord's instructions. The obvious sign of Saul's disobedience was the sound of the Amalekites' sheep and cattle that were still alive. Disobedience is unable to cover its tracks. Samuel pointed out this clear proof of rebellion to the oblivious, unconcerned king.

Saul tried to shift the blame to his soldiers, an old tactic dating back to the garden of Eden (see Gen. 3:12-13). Another timeless method of self-justification was his mixing of truth with a lie. Indeed, they'd destroyed the rest of the flock, but that wasn't what God sought. Finally, Saul attempted to cloak his transgression with the veneer of religiosity, claiming he'd preserved the animals to provide a sacrifice to the Lord.

It's interesting that Saul claimed to be so concerned about offering sacrifice to the Lord after he'd just arrived from a trip arranged to build a statue in honor of himself. Before we attempt to deceive others, we often deceive ourselves. First John 1:8 points out that denying personal sin is actually self-deception.

GOD'S REJECTION (1 Samuel 15:22-23)

BIBLE SKILL
*Use a Bible dictionary
(either print or online)
to learn more about the
historical background.*

Use a Bible dictionary to
discover the history of
the Amalekites.

Notice the different
interactions and
altercations between
them and the Israelites.

How does their
history help you better
understand the conflict
between the two
nations?

²²Then Samuel said: Does the LORD take pleasure in burnt offerings and sacrifices as much as in obeying the LORD? Look: to obey is better than sacrifice, to pay attention is better than the fat of rams.

After a pointed exchange with the king, Samuel asked a rhetorical question for the ages. The obvious answer is no. Obedience is the motive behind any offering of sacrifice, and it's the more crucial response God seeks from us.

*How does accepting partial obedience or religious practice
as a substitute for full obedience show disrespect for God?*

The pleasure of the Lord should be our highest aspiration. Pleasing God results in eternal blessing, while pleasing others or ourselves is a fleeting attainment. Jesus set a high example when He said, "The One who sent Me is with Me. He has not left Me alone, because I always do what pleases Him" (John 8:29).

Samuel used a Hebrew word of exclamation to begin a memorable prophetic utterance. The Hebrew word *hinneh (look)* in 1 Samuel 15:22 is a call to give strong, careful consideration to a matter, in this case the Hebrew practice of faith: to obey is better than sacrifice. In the original language it's only three words, which could be literally translated, "Obedience surpasses sacrifice." Ultimately, obedience is the highest honor we give to God. In obeying His directives, we demonstrate our confidence that His way is the best way. Obedience expresses dependence on Him, affirming that He's truly Lord of all.

²³For rebellion is like the sin of divination, and defiance is like wickedness and idolatry. Because you have rejected the word of the LORD, He has rejected you as king.

The prophet zeroed in on the real crux of Saul's disobedience as rebellion against God. When we disobey God, we defy Him and refuse to honor Him as sovereign and supreme. Disobedience is serious enough for Samuel to liken it to the sin of divination, the unauthorized cavorting with the demonic spirit world. This defiance can also be compared to idolatry, the worship of other gods. In disobedience we make ourselves our own god. Divination and idolatry are the most heinous sins of the Old Testament. When Samuel told Saul what he'd done was the equivalent of these, he meant the deed was inexcusable.

What's the connection between disobedience and idolatry? How do they derive their existence from each other?

Samuel announced a specific, dreadful penalty, which was the verdict rendered by God. Saul's disobedience was a rejection of God's Word. Anytime we refuse to practice what Scripture commands, we set it aside as either untrue or unimportant. In effect we pass judgment on God's edict. Because of Saul's verdict on the instructions of God, the Lord's verdict was handed down on his kingship. Saul would continue to serve in the position of king for many years, but in the eyes of God, on that fateful day at Gilgal, his reign was over.

There may be an interval of time between God's announcement of judgment and its arrival, but it's certain nonetheless. Scoffers may mock the notion of judgment to come because of its delayed arrival (see 2 Pet. 3:4-9), but they'll be proved tragically wrong. The only preparation for judgment is to believe and obey Jesus Christ and His gospel.

❯ OBEY THE TEXT

God expects complete obedience to His directives. Believers are to humbly confront leaders who blatantly disobey God. God is more concerned about obedience than our worship practices.

Review your life, looking for areas of partial obedience. What actions do you need to take to complete your obedience to God?

Discuss as a group the best way to deal with a leader whose disobedience is evident to all. Focus on the actions taken by Samuel to serve as a starting place. How would you want to be confronted if you were a disobedient leader?

Examine your motives for worship and religious activities. Ask God to reveal actions you take that are substitutes for complete obedience to Him.

MEMORIZE

"Samuel said: Does the LORD take pleasure in burnt offerings and sacrifices as much as in obeying the LORD? Look: to obey is better than sacrifice, to pay attention is better than the fat of rams." 1 Samuel 15:22

USE THE SPACE PROVIDED TO MAKE OBSERVATIONS AND RECORD PRAYER
REQUESTS DURING THE GROUP EXPERIENCE FOR THIS SESSION.

MY THOUGHTS

Record insights and questions from the group experience.

_____

_____

_____

_____

_____

_____

MY RESPONSE

Note specific ways you'll put into practice the truth explored this week.

_____

_____

_____

_____

_____

_____

MY PRAYERS

List specific prayer needs and answers to remember this week.

_____

_____

_____

_____

_____

_____

ANOINTED

God desires people who seek to follow Him with all their hearts.

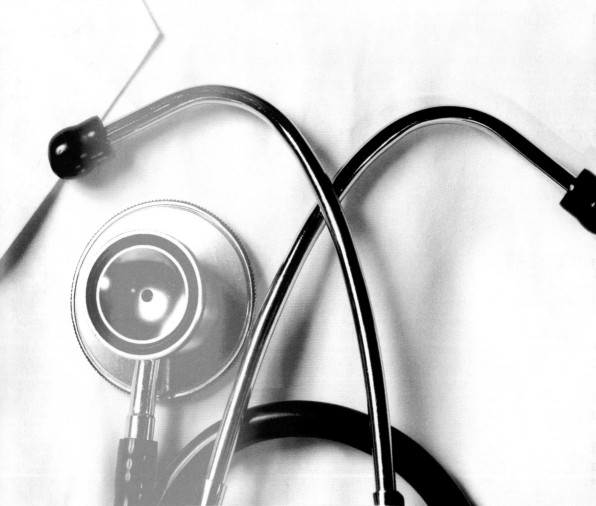

❯ UNDERSTAND THE CONTEXT

Saul's fall no doubt had a profound impact on Samuel. He would have to overcome his grief over Saul before God could use him to move the nation toward a new leader. A dose of reality was part of God's prescription: "I have rejected him as king over Israel" (1 Sam. 16:1). The Lord reminded Samuel of what he already knew: the kingship of Saul was finished. Though Samuel would never again visit Saul (see 15:35), the king occupied a large place in the prophet's thoughts. No doubt Samuel held affection for Saul in spite of his misdeeds.

No matter how Samuel might have felt toward Saul, their final parting exhibited a degree of friction. Samuel performed the deed Saul should have done (see vv. 32-33). As someone who was sensitive to public perception (see v. 30)—though he should have been more concerned with the Lord's honor—Saul was exposed and perhaps embarrassed by Samuel's actions. It isn't hard to imagine that Saul's later paranoia toward David began to emerge at that time with Samuel. At least the prophet suspected as much (see 16:2).

God commanded Samuel to anoint a successor to Saul. As before with His guidance toward Saul, the Lord's initial direction of Samuel was general. All Samuel knew was that the new king would come from Bethlehem and would be a son of a man named Jesse. Because he trusted God, the prophet would be used in what would become a high watermark of his ministry, the anointing of Israel's greatest king.

"ALL THAT IS GOLD

DOES NOT GLITTER."

—J. R. R. TOLKIEN

> 1 SAMUEL 16:4-13

Think About It

What expectations do you see expressed or suggested in these verses? What biases, if any, are expressed?

4 Samuel did what the LORD directed and went to Bethlehem. When the elders of the town met him, they trembled and asked, "Do you come in peace?" **5** "In peace," he replied. "I've come to sacrifice to the LORD. Consecrate yourselves and come with me to the sacrifice." Then he consecrated Jesse and his sons and invited them to the sacrifice. **6** When they arrived, Samuel saw Eliab and said, "Certainly the LORD's anointed one is here before Him." **7** But the LORD said to Samuel, "Do not look at his appearance or his stature, because I have rejected him. Man does not see what the LORD sees, for man sees what is visible, but the LORD sees the heart." **8** Jesse called Abinadab and presented him to Samuel. "The LORD hasn't chosen this one either," Samuel said. **9** Then Jesse presented Shammah, but Samuel said, "The LORD hasn't chosen this one either." **10** After Jesse presented seven of his sons to him, Samuel told Jesse, "The LORD hasn't chosen any of these." **11** Samuel asked him, "Are these all the sons you have?" "There is still the youngest," he answered, "but right now he's tending the sheep." Samuel told Jesse, "Send for him. We won't sit down to eat until he gets here." **12** So Jesse sent for him. He had beautiful eyes and a healthy, handsome appearance. Then the LORD said, "Anoint him, for he is the one." **13** So Samuel took the horn of oil, anointed him in the presence of his brothers, and the Spirit of the LORD took control of David from that day forward. Then Samuel set out and went to Ramah.

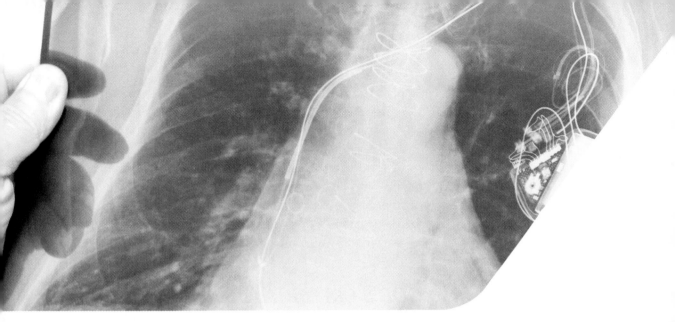

❯ EXPLORE THE TEXT

SAMUEL'S ASSIGNMENT (1 Samuel 16:4-5)

⁴Samuel did what the LORD directed and went to Bethlehem. When the elders of the town met him, they trembled and asked, "Do you come in peace?"

Though the Lord asked a dangerous thing of Samuel (going to Bethlehem would have required him to pass through Gibeah, Saul's town), he complied and went to Bethlehem. He did what Saul failed to do on several occasions—the Lord's will. Samuel's arrival provoked a fearful response on the part of the local leaders, perhaps due to a perception of a growing schism between Saul and Samuel. While the prophet was respected, the king possessed the military power. The elders might also have been afraid because of Samuel's recent execution of King Agag. Serving as God's spokesman is a lonely existence because people both misunderstand you and place you on a pedestal. While they obviously admired and revered the prophet, they were also uncomfortable in his presence.

In what ways does pursuing the call of God on one's life bring isolation from others? What are the risks and rewards of such a pursuit?

⁵"In peace," he replied. "I've come to sacrifice to the LORD. Consecrate yourselves and come with me to the sacrifice." Then he consecrated Jesse and his sons and invited them to the sacrifice.

Samuel assured the people that his intentions toward Bethlehem were peaceful, explaining that his purpose was to offer a sacrifice to the Lord. Such a time of worship required preparation and cleansing. Such consecration would have involved certain rituals and abstinence from certain activities (see Ex. 19:9-15). Old Testament worship regulations point to Christ (see Heb. 9:10-14), teaching the necessity of preparing oneself for worship. Samuel prepared Jesse and his sons for the sacrifice. Christ does the same for us. God requires purity of heart in those who approach Him in worship (see 10:19-22).

GOD'S CRITERIA (1 Samuel 16:6-10)

⁶When they arrived, Samuel saw Eliab and said, "Certainly the LORD's anointed one is here before Him."

As the sacrificial ceremony began, Samuel saw Jesse's oldest son, Eliab, and he was favorably impressed. We learn in the next verse that Eliab was tall, a quality Saul also possessed (see 10:23). The prophet seemed confident that Eliab was the one chosen by God to become the king.

What dangers lie in assuming that certain individuals are suited for leadership based on appearance or a generalization?

⁷But the LORD said to Samuel, "Do not look at his appearance or his stature, because I have rejected him. Man does not see what the LORD sees, for man sees what is visible, but the LORD sees the heart."

Though it is likely that Eliab was later a leader in the tribe of Judah, he was not the Lord's choice for the earthly throne of Israel. The Lord often chooses those the world deems undesirable as a way to bring honor to Himself (see 1 Cor. 1:26-29).

The Lord reminded Samuel that He's different from man because He can assess more than a person's outward appearance. God perfectly knows the heart, that is to say, a person's values, motives, and deepest convictions. Eliab may have been a true worshiper of Yahweh—and he probably was—but there was something missing at the core of his being for which God was looking.

⁸Jesse called Abinadab and presented him to Samuel. "The LORD hasn't chosen this one either," Samuel said. ⁹Then Jesse presented Shammah, but Samuel said, "The LORD hasn't chosen this one either."

Abinadab, the second son of Jesse, was also summoned to come before Samuel. Because the Lord had corrected Samuel's superficial evaluation, the prophet was able to discern that neither was Abinadab the Lord's chosen king. The scenario repeated itself with Shammah, the third in birth order of Jesse's sons. None of the top candidates were the Lord's choice. More frequently than we might realize, God rejects our human pecking order in calling a leader.

What criteria do we use to select our leaders? How does God's choice open the door for Him to be honored?

¹⁰After Jesse presented seven of his sons to him, Samuel told Jesse, "The LORD hasn't chosen any of these."

Seven of Jesse's sons were rejected as the future king of God's people. We can only imagine the awkward silence in the air that day. We can only wonder what might have been going on in the heart of Samuel. He was obedient to the Lord and committed to the task of appointing Israel's next king, but all his efforts had been fruitless up to this point.

The human tendency is sometimes simply to settle for someone to fill an empty office or role. We can grow anxious in our search for spiritual leaders or even spouses; as a result, we make a premature choice. To his credit, Samuel waited for the Lord's guidance, and we should do the same.

DAVID'S SELECTION (1 Samuel 16:11-13)

¹¹Samuel asked him, "Are these all the sons you have?" "There is still the youngest," he answered, "but right now he's tending the sheep." Samuel told Jesse, "Send for him. We won't sit down to eat until he gets here."

BIBLE SKILL
Read for emphasis.

Read aloud 1 Samuel 16:7 several times, placing emphasis on different words or phrases with each reading.

You may want to emphasize nouns, then verbs, and then prepositional phrases.

Record ways each reading gives a different insight into the verse.

Samuel found himself in a very real dilemma. He'd been obedient to the Lord's guidance, and yet his experience wasn't in line with the revelation he'd received. But the prophet didn't lose heart. His faith prompted him to keep seeking and to ask Jesse if he had any other sons.

Jesse replied that indeed there was another son. Samuel received Jesse's words hopefully and commanded that the boy who'd been caring for the sheep be summoned. Someone had to watch the sheep, so perhaps this was a reason for the initial exclusion.

The image of a shepherd-leader is prevalent throughout the Old Testament Scriptures (see Ps. 78:72; Jer. 3:15), partly because it's a picture of the way God led His people (see Pss. 23; 100:3; Ezek. 34:11-16). Perhaps an early predictor of Saul's incompetency as a leader was seen in his ineptness as a shepherd, unable to find his father's animals that had wandered off (see 1 Sam. 9:3-4). It's even more likely that this reference to a son of Jesse who shepherded the flock would foreshadow a king of Israel who would lead God's people (see 2 Sam. 5:1-2; 7:8).

What similarities exist between a shepherd and an effective leader?

Perhaps it was because this absent son of Jesse was so young that he wasn't included in this adult gathering. Samuel was adamant that this youngest son join them for the meal associated with the sacrifice. A reader can almost sense the hope rising in Samuel's heart that Saul's successor could still be found among the sons of Jesse.

12So Jesse sent for him. He had beautiful eyes and a healthy, handsome appearance. Then the LORD said, "Anoint him, for he is the one." 13So Samuel took the horn of oil, anointed him in the presence of his brothers, and the Spirit of the LORD took control of David from that day forward. Then Samuel set out and went to Ramah.

Samuel demonstrated before everyone present the Lord's selection of David as king by pouring oil over him. This selection was the work of God (see 2 Sam. 23:1); Samuel was merely the instrument. Anointing with oil was a symbol of the work of the Holy Spirit and His coming on an individual (see Isa. 61:1). Through the Spirit, David would lead the people of God, bringing justice to the entire nation (see 2 Sam. 8:15). Even when David sinned, he understood his need for the Holy Spirit and the presence of God in his life (see Ps. 51:11).

Samuel anointed David in Bethlehem (1 Sam. 16:4). Bethlehem would be important for God's people not only in Samuel's day but also in days to come. The prophet Micah would point to Bethlehem as the birthplace of the promised Messiah. Centuries later that prophecy was fulfilled with the birth of Jesus Christ, God's Anointed One (see John 1:41) who's our perfect King (see Matt. 2:1-6).

Only a few individuals in the Old Testament were empowered by the Holy Spirit. However, the Spirit today baptizes every believer in Christ into His body, the church (see 1 Cor. 12:13). Though He was in the midst of God's people in the Old Testament (see Hag. 2:5), the Spirit indwells each believer today (see 1 Cor. 6:19).

On a scale of 1 to 10, how important is it for leaders to be sensitive and responsive to the Holy Spirit? Would you consider their willingness to follow Him as a requirement for being an effective leader? Explain.

❯ OBEY THE TEXT

God chooses leaders for His people. At times believers' motives are more important than their actions. When we're called on to lead, we can trust the Holy Spirit for guidance.

Outline the process used by your group and church for selecting leaders. How is God's direction incorporated into the process? How do you seek God's direction for the process?

Examine your motives for your involvement or leadership in any ministry area. Ask God to reveal any motives that need to be brought in line with His purposes. What do you need to do so that God can purify the motives of your heart?

How can your group encourage your pastor as he seeks the guidance of the Holy Spirit for the church? Discuss options as a group and adopt at least one action for encouraging your pastor and other leaders to remain faithful to God's direction.

MEMORIZE

"The Lᴏʀᴅ said to Samuel, 'Do not look at his appearance or his stature, because I have rejected him. Man does not see what the Lᴏʀᴅ sees, for man sees what is visible, but the Lᴏʀᴅ sees the heart.' " 1 Samuel 16:7

USE THE SPACE PROVIDED TO MAKE OBSERVATIONS AND RECORD PRAYER
REQUESTS DURING THE GROUP EXPERIENCE FOR THIS SESSION.

MY THOUGHTS

Record insights and questions from the group experience.

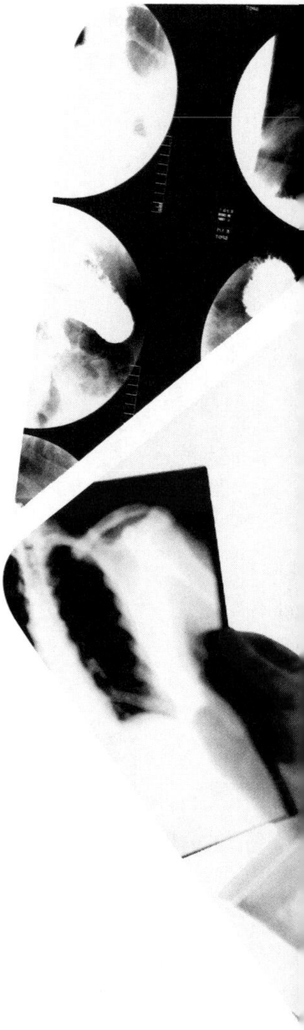

_____
_____
_____
_____
_____
_____

MY RESPONSE

Note specific ways you'll put into practice the truth explored this week.

_____
_____
_____
_____
_____
_____

MY PRAYERS

List specific prayer needs and answers to remember this week.

_____
_____
_____
_____
_____
_____

DELIVERED

God uses faithful servants to deliver His people.

❯ UNDERSTAND THE CONTEXT

Context in the Bible is crucial. Not only does it set the scene, but it also establishes themes and patterns in the text. A major theme in 1 Samuel is faithful leadership. The leadership of Israel transitioned from judges (Eli and Samuel) to kings (Saul and David). Eli and Samuel are considered to be the last two judges; Saul and David are the first two kings. Regardless of our title in the kingdom of God, He wants us to be faithful.

In this session we'll see how God uses faithful servants to deliver His people. One truth will be very clear: God employs and empowers faithfulness. He doesn't require brilliance, He doesn't need human strength, and He isn't impressed by status.

David was faithful in simple tasks, such as watching sheep and taking supplies to his brothers. Ironically, it was his faithfulness in simple tasks that put him in situations where he had to trust God in major ways. If David hadn't been watching the sheep, he wouldn't have encountered the bear or the lion (see 1 Sam. 17:34-36). If David hadn't taken supplies to his brothers, he never would have heard Goliath's taunts (see v. 23). Faithfulness in simple tasks can put us in situations where we have to trust God in major ways.

"IT IS CURIOUS THAT PHYSICAL COURAGE SHOULD BE SO COMMON IN THE WORLD AND MORAL COURAGE SO RARE."
—Mark Twain

> 1 SAMUEL 17:32-37,42-50

Think About It

Look in these verses for specific examples of trusting God and faithfully serving Him. If you defined heroism by these qualities, how would that change your perspective on everyday tasks?

32 David said to Saul, "Don't let anyone be discouraged by him; your servant will go and fight this Philistine!" **33** But Saul replied, "You can't go fight this Philistine. You're just a youth, and he's been a warrior since he was young." **34** David answered Saul: "Your servant has been tending his father's sheep. Whenever a lion or a bear came and carried off a lamb from the flock, **35** I went after it, struck it down, and rescued the lamb from its mouth. If it reared up against me, I would grab it by its fur, strike it down, and kill it. **36** Your servant has killed lions and bears; this uncircumcised Philistine will be like one of them, for he has defied the armies of the living God." **37** Then David said, "The LORD who rescued me from the paw of the lion and the paw of the bear will rescue me from the hand of this Philistine." Saul said to David, "Go, and may the LORD be with you."

42 When the Philistine looked and saw David, he despised him because he was just a youth, healthy and handsome. **43** He said to David, "Am I a dog that you come against me with sticks?" Then he cursed David by his gods. **44** "Come here," the Philistine called to David, "and I'll give your flesh to the birds of the sky and the wild beasts!" **45** David said to the Philistine: "You come against me with a dagger, spear, and sword, but I come against you in the name of Yahweh of Hosts, the God of Israel's armies—you have defied Him. **46** Today, the LORD will hand you over to me. Today, I'll strike you down, cut your head off, and give the corpses of the Philistine camp to the birds of the sky and the creatures of the earth. Then all the world will know that Israel has a God, **47** and this whole assembly will know that it is not by sword or by spear that the LORD saves, for the battle is the LORD's. He will hand you over to us." **48** When the Philistine started forward to attack him, David ran quickly to the battle line to meet the Philistine. **49** David put his hand in the bag, took out a stone, slung it, and hit the Philistine on his forehead. The stone sank into his forehead, and he fell on his face to the ground. **50** David defeated the Philistine with a sling and a stone. Even though David had no sword, he struck down the Philistine and killed him.

❯ EXPLORE THE TEXT

CONFIDENCE IN GOD *(1 Samuel 17:32-37)*

³²David said to Saul, "Don't let anyone be discouraged by him; your servant will go and fight this Philistine!" ³³But Saul replied, "You can't go fight this Philistine. You're just a youth, and he's been a warrior since he was young."

There's a major difference between prideful confidence and godly confidence. Prideful confidence believes I can do it. I'm able. I'll make it work. The emphasis is on self. Godly confidence believes God is able. God is sovereign. God is victorious. The emphasis is on God. Scripture teaches us to trust in God's ability, not our own (see 1 Chron. 29:11-12; Ps. 135:6; Prov. 3:5-6). While Philippians 4:13 says, "I am able to do all things through Him who strengthens me," the emphasis is clearly on "Him who strengthens me." Jesus removed all doubt when He said, "You can do nothing without Me" (John 15:5).

David was confident that God would bring victory. Goliath didn't taunt just any army; he taunted "the armies of the living God" (1 Sam. 17:26). In spite of the incredible odds against him, David had faith that victory is always in God's hands.

Even though David was confident, Saul had doubts. David was just a youth, while the Philistine had been a warrior since he was young. Seeing the differences in age, experience, size, and preparedness, Saul thought the fight would be over before it started. From a physical perspective the odds were definitely in Goliath's favor. From a spiritual perspective, however, Goliath never stood a chance.

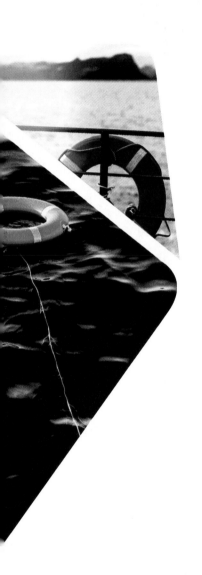

Saul questioned David's experience in battle. How could David's lack of battle experience have been a disadvantage? How could it have been an advantage?

³⁴David answered Saul: "Your servant has been tending his father's sheep. Whenever a lion or a bear came and carried off a lamb from the flock, ³⁵I went after it, struck it down, and rescued the lamb from its mouth. If it reared up against me, I would grab it by its fur, strike it down, and kill it."

To convince Saul, David shared that God had previously enabled him to kill a lion and a bear. Let that thought sink in for just a moment. Very few people survive an attack by a lion or a bear. Apart from this account, have you ever heard of someone surviving an attack by both? The fraternity for lion and bear survivors has to be small.

David didn't enter that fraternity by choice but by necessity. He was a shepherd (see 16:11; 17:15), charged with tending his father's sheep. The primary duties of a shepherd are to guide, sustain, and protect the flock. Protecting the flock is a full-time job. Sheep are accident-prone and easy targets for dangerous animals and robbers.

David's courage was remarkable. If the average person saw a lion or a bear carry off a lamb, he would probably write it off as a loss. David actually "went after it, struck it down, and rescued the lamb from its mouth" (v. 35). The language suggests not only a willingness to protect the sheep but also an eagerness to take the fight to the enemy.

The final part of verse 35 is also incredible. "By its fur" can also be translated "by his beard" or "by the chin." Two ancient translations, the Chaldee and Septuagint, translate the phrase as "the lower jaw" and "the throat" respectively. The picture is pretty clear. David grabbed the lion and the bear by their necks and killed them.

³⁶"Your servant has killed lions and bears; this uncircumcised Philistine will be like one of them, for he has defied the armies of the living God." ³⁷Then David said, "The LORD who rescued me from the paw of the lion and the paw of the bear will rescue me from the hand of this Philistine." Saul said to David, "Go, and may the LORD be with you."

David drew from God's past faithfulness to argue for God's faithfulness in the future. God rescued David from the hand of the lion and the bear, and He would rescue him from the hand of this Philistine.

Saul had the power to reject David's offer and find another warrior. For that matter, Saul could have fought Goliath himself. Based on former descriptions of Saul, he was literally head and shoulders taller than most people (see 9:2). But David made a compelling case. His insistence on God's past protection was instrumental in changing Saul's mind.

Although it might seem cowardly for Saul to send David into the fight, his decision was somewhat courageous. The conditions of the combat were extreme. If David lost the fight, the Israelites would become the servants of the Philistines (see 17:9). Saul needed a strong level of confidence in David's ability to fight. David's loss would have had an impact on the whole nation.

How can God use our past as a foundation for our future?
How can our past experiences help us succeed in the future?

FALSE CONFIDENCE IN SELF
(1 Samuel 17:42-44)

⁴²**When the Philistine looked and saw David, he despised him because he was just a youth, healthy and handsome. ⁴³He said to David, "Am I a dog that you come against me with sticks?" Then he cursed David by his gods. ⁴⁴"Come here," the Philistine called to David, "and I'll give your flesh to the birds of the sky and the wild beasts!"**

David was confident that God would prevail. Goliath was confident that his own abilities were unmatched. The Philistine probably felt invincible, based on his size and experience. Goliath's pride was hurt when he saw that the youth David was his competition.

The Philistine either overlooked David's sling or discounted the sling's ability to inflict any real harm. Instead, he focused on the staff in David's hand. The implication is that a stick might be appropriate for

KEY DOCTRINE
The Kingdom

The kingdom of God includes both His general sovereignty over the universe and His particular kingship over people who willfully acknowledge Him as King.

beating a dog (the lowest of animals; see 1 Sam. 24:14; 2 Sam. 3:8; 9:8; 16:9), but it's insufficient for stopping a champion. Goliath continued his verbal assault when he cursed David. If Goliath's size weren't intimidating enough, his psychological assault could elicit fear.

In what items or people do we sometimes place our confidence? What are the limits of each item or person? How do those limits point to our need to trust in God at all times with all things?

GOD'S VICTORY *(1 Samuel 17:45-50)*

⁴⁵**David said to the Philistine: "You come against me with a dagger, spear, and sword, but I come against you in the name of Yahweh of Hosts, the God of Israel's armies—you have defied Him. ⁴⁶Today, the LORD will hand you over to me. Today, I'll strike you down, cut your head off, and give the corpses of the Philistine camp to the birds of the sky and the creatures of the earth. Then all the world will know that Israel has a God, ⁴⁷and this whole assembly will know that it is not by sword or by spear that the LORD saves, for the battle is the LORD's. He will hand you over to us."**

Humility and confidence aren't mutually exclusive terms. It's possible to walk humbly while brimming with confidence in God. David was confident in God's ability to act through him. In verse 46 David claimed the victory, predicted the timeline, shared the consequences, and verbalized the stakes. David turned many of Goliath's arguments back on the giant.

If David's taunts seem prideful in any way, his motives should clarify any confusion. David wasn't fighting for personal gain or glory. David wanted all people to recognize the God of Israel and to know that He delivers His people. God doesn't need weapons of war (see Ps. 44:3-7) or the power of people (see Zech. 4:6). God is the sovereign Deliverer, and the battle is the Lord's. Every challenge, trial, and problem is an opportunity for God to show Himself strong before the world.

BIBLE SKILL
Compare and contrast passages with related themes.

Read Luke 2:41-50 and Luke 4:1-13, identifying actions that prepared Jesus as a leader.

Compare these actions with the actions David took to prepare to be a leader.

What's unique?

What's similar?

What role did David's and Jesus' relationships with the Father play in their preparation for leadership?

⁴⁸When the Philistine started forward to attack him, David ran quickly to the battle line to meet the Philistine. ⁴⁹David put his hand in the bag, took out a stone, slung it, and hit the Philistine on his forehead. The stone sank into his forehead, and he fell on his face to the ground. ⁵⁰David defeated the Philistine with a sling and a stone. Even though David had no sword, he struck down the Philistine and killed him.

The verbal assaults gave way to physical confrontation. Goliath moved closer to attack. David quickly ran to meet him in the same way he'd gone after the lion and the bear (see v. 35). He reached into his bag, grabbed a stone, and slung it with such deadly force that it crushed Goliath's frontal bone and sank into his forehead. Goliath fell on his face to the ground. The scene is reminiscent of the way Dagon fell on his face before the ark of the Lord (see 5:4).

With a stone, a sling, and a faithful servant, God delivered His people from their enemies. We must also recognize that this account ultimately points to Jesus, the representative leader of His people. Jesus faced and defeated the giants of sin and death on our behalf. On the cross He delivered us from an enemy we were powerless to defeat ourselves.

How has God brought victory in your life when you were powerless in your own ability?

❯ OBEY THE TEXT

God calls faithful followers to take a stand against those who oppose Him and His people. Confidence in anything other than God will ultimately lead to sure defeat. God gives His followers opportunities to make His name known.

In what ways are you being called on to stand with God? What actions can you take to make sure God receives honor in the process?

Examine your life, looking for areas in which you're more likely to depend on yourself than on God. Ask God to forgive you for not fully depending on Him. Ask Him for strength and humility to do so in the future.

Discuss with your Bible-study group ways you can actively make known in your community God's name and His offer of redemption through His Son. Identify actions the group can take to be more actively engaged in sharing the good news of Jesus.

MEMORIZE

"Today, the LORD will hand you over to me. Today, I'll strike you down, cut your head off, and give the corpses of the Philistine camp to the birds of the sky and the creatures of the earth. Then all the world will know that Israel has a God." 1 Samuel 17:46

USE THE SPACE PROVIDED TO MAKE OBSERVATIONS AND RECORD PRAYER
REQUESTS DURING THE GROUP EXPERIENCE FOR THIS SESSION.

MY THOUGHTS

Record insights and questions from the group experience.

_____
_____
_____
_____
_____
_____
_____

MY RESPONSE

Note specific ways you'll put into practice the truth explored this week.

_____
_____
_____
_____
_____
_____

MY PRAYERS

List specific prayer needs and answers to remember this week.

_____
_____
_____
_____
_____
_____

RESPECT

God is ultimately in charge of those who lead.

❯ UNDERSTAND THE CONTEXT

Because Saul was obsessed with killing David (see 1 Sam. 18:10-17; 19:10; 20:33), David was forced to go into hiding. He and his small army of supporters hid in caves (see 22:1; 24:3), lived in foreign lands (see 27:7), and did whatever was necessary to survive (see 21:1-6). From David's perspective the whole situation must have been somewhat confusing. He was minding his own business when Samuel anointed him as king (see 16:1-13). He was defending God's honor when He defeated Goliath (see 17:1-51). He was serving his king when God blessed him with military success (see 18:2,5). God gave him victories, popularity, and success (see vv. 5,14). So why was he on the run?

David's story speaks to a common misunderstanding. When good things happen, people see them as signs of God's approval. When bad things happen, people see them as signs of God's disapproval. That theory is disproved throughout the Bible. Hebrews 11 recounts the stories of multiple people whom God approved for their faith, but they went through difficult times. Difficulty isn't necessarily a sign of God's disapproval. In fact, God uses difficulty to mature His people.

While hiding in a cave near En-gedi, David was presented with an opportunity to kill Saul, end the persecution, and seize the throne for himself (see 1 Sam. 24:1-7). But he refused to do so. He would wait for God to remove Saul before making any claim to the throne.

A second opportunity to kill Saul presented itself to David in the Wilderness of Ziph (see 26:7-8). Again, David refused to kill Saul. He could have assumed that these opportunities were his reward for righteous living. After all, logic says, "Don't miss the same opportunity twice. God is pleased with you. Take your reward." But faith says, "God's blessings won't compromise God's principles. Circumstances don't indicate God's favor or disapproval. God is your reward."

> "I'M NOT CONCERNED WITH YOUR LIKING OR DISLIKING ME. ALL I ASK IS THAT YOU RESPECT ME AS A HUMAN BEING."
>
> —Jackie Robinson

Think About It

In these passages underline actions or statements that demonstrate respect.

Circle actions or statements that demonstrate humility.

Notice ways respect and humility overlap in this account.

Look for the rationale David gave for his actions. In what way was his respect for people tied to his respect for God?

7 That night, David and Abishai came to the troops, and Saul was lying there asleep in the inner circle of the camp with his spear stuck in the ground by his head. Abner and the troops were lying around him. **8** Then Abishai said to David, "Today God has handed your enemy over to you. Let me thrust the spear through him into the ground just once. I won't have to strike him twice!" **9** But David said to Abishai, "Don't destroy him, for who can lift a hand against the LORD's anointed and be blameless?" **10** David added, "As the LORD lives, the LORD will certainly strike him down: either his day will come and he will die, or he will go into battle and perish. **11** However, because of the LORD, I will never lift my hand against the LORD's anointed. Instead, take the spear and the water jug by his head, and let's go." **12** So David took the spear and the water jug by Saul's head, and they went their way. No one saw them, no one knew, and no one woke up; they all remained asleep because a deep sleep from the LORD came over them.

21 Saul responded, "I have sinned. Come back, my son David, I will never harm you again because today you considered my life precious. I have been a fool! I've committed a grave error." **22** David answered, "Here is the king's spear; have one of the young men come over and get it. **23** May the LORD repay every man for his righteousness and his loyalty. I wasn't willing to lift my hand against the LORD's anointed, even though the LORD handed you over to me today. **24** Just as I considered your life valuable today, so may the LORD consider my life valuable and rescue me from all trouble." **25** Saul said to him, "You are blessed, my son David. You will certainly do great things and will also prevail." Then David went on his way, and Saul returned home.

❯ EXPLORE THE TEXT

OPPORTUNITY KNOCKS (1 Samuel 26:7-8)

⁷That night, David and Abishai came to the troops, and Saul was lying there asleep in the inner circle of the camp with his spear stuck in the ground by his head. Abner and the troops were lying around him. ⁸Then Abishai said to David, "Today God has handed your enemy over to you. Let me thrust the spear through him into the ground just once. I won't have to strike him twice!"

It was reported to Saul that David was hiding on the hill of Hachilah opposite Jeshimon (see v. 1). Saul saw an opportunity to kill his rival and secure his crown. He took three thousand of his best men and searched for David in the Wilderness of Ziph (see v. 2).

Just as Saul received information on David's location, David had spies who knew that Saul had come (see v. 4). When David received the information, he asked two men to go with him to the place where Saul had camped. The first man asked to go was a warrior and mercenary named Ahimelech the Hittite (see v. 6), not to be confused with Ahimelech the priest (see 21:1-9). The second man asked to go was David's nephew, Abishai. Abishai was the only one who went with David.

When David and Abishai entered the camp, Saul and his men were in a deep sleep brought on by the Lord (see 26:12). David and Abishai were able to move about freely without detection. When they came to the place where Saul was sleeping, they saw

his spear stuck in the ground by his head. The spear was Saul's weapon of choice and a symbol of his royal position. Anxious to get rid of Saul and the impending threat that came with him, Abishai wanted to kill him with his own spear.

The scene is similar to the time when David crept up behind Saul in the cave (see 24:4). In both situations David's men considered Saul's defenseless position to be proof that God wanted Saul to die by David's hand.

Hurried decisions are rarely good decisions. Saul was the sovereign king, and David was his loyal subject. Even though Saul's kingdom was doomed (see 13:14), it wasn't David's place to take matters into his own hands. God's ultimate plan didn't require David's involvement. It's also possible that David had already learned a lesson about rushing to kill someone. In the previous chapter God had prevented David from vindicating himself against Nabal (see 25:2-38). David had realized that God had sent Abigail to keep him from bloodshed (see vv. 32-33). Whatever the reason, David didn't harm Saul when it was within his power to do so.

What are the dangers of equating an open door with God's will? How can we know the difference between a true open door and a test disguised as an open door?

GODLY RESPECT *(1 Samuel 26:9-12)*

⁹**But David said to Abishai, "Don't destroy him, for who can lift a hand against the LORD's anointed and be blameless?"** ¹⁰**David added, "As the LORD lives, the LORD will certainly strike him down: either his day will come and he will die, or he will go into battle and perish.** ¹¹**However, because of the LORD, I will never lift my hand against the LORD's anointed. Instead, take the spear and the water jug by his head, and let's go."** ¹²**So David took the spear and the water jug by Saul's head, and they went their way. No one saw them, no one knew, and no one woke up; they all remained asleep because a deep sleep from the LORD came over them.**

While Abishai was willing to kill Saul to help David, David recognized that God had a better way. The earlier encounter with Nabal (see 25:2-38) confirmed the Lord's sovereign judgment in these matters. If David and his men took matters into their own hands, they would be acting against the Lord's anointed. David decided to let God handle the situation. Saul's death would come as a result of the second option David described in 26:10 (see 31:1-6).

David's respect for Saul may seem illogical from a military perspective, but it was well thought out from a theological perspective. David viewed this situation as an opportunity to use restraint toward one of the Lord's leaders. It wasn't David's place to punish the Lord's servant.

Instead, David chose to make a point. He ordered Abishai to take the spear and the water jug beside Saul's head. The spear was a symbol of his power; the water jug was a symbol of life-sustaining resources. In one gesture they symbolically stripped Saul of his power and his life.

The writer didn't attribute these events to human skill or stealth. Instead, he gave credit to God. God demonstrated His sovereign ability to protect His people and accomplish His purposes.

Respect is often seen as something that must be earned. David showed respect to someone who didn't show respect to him. Why is it hard to respect people who disrespect us? Why should we?

KEY DOCTRINE
Peace and War

The true remedy for the war spirit is the gospel of our Lord.

REMORSE (1 Samuel 26:21)

²¹**Saul responded, "I have sinned. Come back, my son David, I will never harm you again because today you considered my life precious. I have been a fool! I've committed a grave error."**

When there was distance between them (see v. 13), David shouted to Saul's troops and to Abner, the commander of Saul's army (see v. 14), to ask why Abner hadn't protected the king when someone had come to destroy him (see v. 15). David pointed out that the king's spear and water jug were missing (see v. 16). By this time Saul recognized David's voice (see v. 17).

BIBLE SKILL

Compare similar situations.

Read 1 Samuel 13:8-14 and compare Saul's actions with David's actions in 1 Samuel 26.

What do these passages reveal about each man's character?

How do these two passages illustrate the value of patience and the danger of impatience?

After Saul verified that it was David, David asked Saul why he was pursuing him (see v. 18). David was trying to understand his offense. Recognizing that David spared his life once again, Saul admitted that he had sinned.

Saul's admission of guilt was different from his admission of guilt recorded in 24:17-21. In chapter 24 Saul had been amazed that David would spare his enemy's life, and he'd asked David not to cut off his descendants. In 26:21, however, Saul confessed that he'd sinned. He wasn't just frustrated that his soldiers hadn't been able to protect him; he was vexed that he had sinned, been a fool, and "committed a grave error." Saul asked David to come back with him and promised never to harm him again.

True repentance comes when God convicts a person of sin (see John 16:8). When have you been made aware of your sin? How did you respond?

TRUST IN GOD (1 Samuel 26:22-25)

22David answered, "Here is the king's spear; have one of the young men come over and get it. 23May the LORD repay every man for his righteousness and his loyalty. I wasn't willing to lift my hand against the LORD's anointed, even though the LORD handed you over to me today. 24Just as I considered your life valuable today, so may the LORD consider my life valuable and rescue me from all trouble." 25Saul said to him, "You are blessed, my son David. You will certainly do great things and will also prevail." Then David went on his way, and Saul returned home.

David's response to Saul's admission of sin was cautious at best. He offered to return Saul's spear (a symbol of death), but he chose to keep Saul's jug (a symbol of life). Even when returning the spear, David was cautious. Saul seemed to relent, but David placed no confidence in Saul's promise.

David wasn't willing to lift his hand against the Lord's anointed. He trusted that the Lord would value his life and rescue him from all trouble. David valued Saul's life, but he didn't ask Saul to reciprocate. Instead, he placed his life in God's hands and prayed for God's deliverance from all trouble.

Saul, in his final words to David, offered good wishes wrapped in relational overtones. Saul called David son three times (see 1 Sam. 26:17,21,25). He also seemed to recognize that David would be his successor as king.

Sin had been confessed. Remorse had been shown. Questions had been asked. Promises had been made. At this point there was nothing else to be said. David went on his way, and Saul returned home. David and Saul parted ways, and they never saw each other alive again. This was the last recorded conversation between David and Saul.

How can you show respect to people while also being cautious to place your ultimate trust in God?

❯ OBEY THE TEXT

Opportunities must be weighed in light of God's principles and will. God expects His followers to respect the lives of others, even those who oppose them. God's timing can be trusted in all matters of life.

What open doors are presently in front of you? What steps are you taking to determine which doors are within God's will?

Identify individuals whom you have difficulty respecting. What steps can you take to move beyond any past experiences and begin to develop respect for each person identified?

As a group, discuss the correlation between humility and respect. How does humility promote respect? In what ways is God calling you to humble yourself before others? How does your group encourage humility and respect among the group members?

MEMORIZE

"David said to Abishai, 'Don't destroy him, for who can lift a hand against the LORD's anointed and be blameless?' " 1 Samuel 26:9

USE THE SPACE PROVIDED TO MAKE OBSERVATIONS AND RECORD PRAYER
REQUESTS DURING THE GROUP EXPERIENCE FOR THIS SESSION.

MY THOUGHTS

Record insights and questions from the group experience.

_____
_____
_____
_____
_____
_____

MY RESPONSE

Note specific ways you'll put into practice the truth explored this week.

_____
_____
_____
_____
_____
_____

MY PRAYERS

List specific prayer needs and answers to remember this week.

_____
_____
_____
_____
_____
_____

❯ GETTING STARTED

OPENING OPTIONS: Choose one of the following to open the group discussion.

WEEKLY QUOTATION DISCUSSION STARTER: "I have so much to do that I shall spend the first three hours in prayer."—Martin Luther

> ❯ What's your initial response to this week's quotation?

> ❯ What steps do you take to bring order to your day and to identify priorities?

> ❯ Today we'll see that making prayer a priority enables us to focus on God's ability to accomplish what's beyond our own abilities.

CREATIVE ACTIVITY: Before the group meets, get a three-pack can of tennis balls. With all the balls in the can, carefully pour uncooked rice into the can, filling the space between the tennis balls until the can is full. Then pour the rice back into a separate container. When the group arrives, use the following demonstration and questions.

> ❯ This empty can represents the amount of time we have. The tennis balls represent priorities like worship, community, and prayer. The rice represents our other obligations and activities.

> ❯ Ask people to provide examples of typical activities in their lives, such as work, family, and exercise. Pour rice into the empty can with each answer until all the rice is in the can.

> ❯ Place the three tennis balls on top of the rice, revealing that they won't all fit and that something important will be left out.

> ❯ Remove everything from the can and then place the tennis balls in the empty can first. Now pour the rice into the can, revealing that everything now fits into the same space.

> ❯ Today we'll see that prioritizing prayer, worship, and godly community allows us to see God do things that are otherwise impossible.

❯ UNDERSTAND THE CONTEXT

PROVIDE BACKGROUND: Briefly introduce members to 1 Samuel, pointing out the major themes and any information that will help them understand 1 Samuel 1:10-18,26-28 (see pp. 7 and 9). Then, to help people personally connect today's context with the original context, use the following questions and statements.

> ❯ About what kinds of things do you most often pray?

> ❯ Why is prayer vital to a person's relationship with God?

> ❯ The Book of 1 Samuel opens with the prayers of a woman named Hannah.

❯ EXPLORE THE TEXT

READ THE BIBLE: Ask two volunteers to read 1 Samuel 1:10-18,26-28.

DISCUSS: Use the following questions to discuss group members' initial reactions to the text.

> Why might it be significant that the Book of 1 Samuel opens with a story of prayer and provision?

> How does the text describe Hannah's emotions? What does this passage reveal about emotional honesty in our spiritual lives?

> How does specific prayer function in this story? Godly counsel? Worship?

> How did Eli respond before understanding the situation? After understanding? After God answered?

> What can we conclude from the change in Hannah's behavior after her prayer but before God's answer?

> What else does this text teach us about God? Ourselves?

> What other questions or observations do you have?

NOTE: Provide ample time for group members to share responses and questions about the text. Don't feel pressured to prioritize the printed agenda over group members' personal experiences. If time allows, discuss responses to the questions in the personal reading.

❯ OBEY THE TEXT

RESPOND: Foster an environment of openness and action. Help individuals apply biblical truth to specific areas of personal thought, attitude, and/or behavior.

> Are you ever afraid to make specific requests in prayer? Why or why not?

> Who can share a story of God's answering a specific prayer immediately or over time?

> How do today's study and the stories just shared encourage you?

> What will you do to start prioritizing prayer as a regular part of your week?

> How can we pray for one another now and throughout the week?

PRAY: Close by praying for group members to desire and rely on daily time in prayer. Ask God to work on behalf of any requests shared. Thank God that He hears us and answers our prayers in His timing.

GETTING STARTED

OPENING OPTIONS: Choose one of the following to open the group discussion.

WEEKLY QUOTATION DISCUSSION STARTER: "God has set apart His people from before the foundation of the world to be His chosen and peculiar inheritance."—Charles Spurgeon

> What's your initial response to this week's quotation?

> In what ways are Christians to be set apart from and peculiar in today's culture?

> Today we'll see how Israel turned from God and desired conformity to the world.

CREATIVE ACTIVITY: Before the group session secure a video clip similar to clips on shows like "America's Funniest Videos," in which people do things that prove to be bad ideas in humorous ways. After the group arrives, show the video clip and use the following statements and questions for discussion.

> We can all identify with embarrassing moments when things go wrong. It's easy to laugh at others, knowing we all have bad moments, but it's not always funny at the time, and sometimes it can have serious consequences.

> When have you done something that backfired or severely disappointed you or someone else?

> Did you know it might be a bad idea, or did someone warn you?

> Why did you insist on doing it anyway?

> Today we'll see Israel's stubborn insistence despite warnings and implied consequences.

UNDERSTAND THE CONTEXT

PROVIDE BACKGROUND: Briefly introduce members to major themes, information, and ideas that will help them understand 1 Samuel 8:4-9,19-22 (see p. 17). Then, to help people personally connect today's context with the original context, use the following questions and statements.

> When have you experienced a personal transition? Was it for the better or worse?

> What transitions have you seen in our culture? Are they for the better or worse?

> In today's study we'll see the people of Israel begin to transition from a theocracy— a nation ruled by God—to a monarchy—a nation ruled by a king.

❯ EXPLORE THE TEXT

READ THE BIBLE: Ask two volunteers to read 1 Samuel 8:4-9,19-22.

DISCUSS: Use the following questions to discuss group members' initial reactions to the text.

> What reasons did the people give for wanting a king? What desires did their reasoning reveal? What fears were revealed?

> Why did Samuel consider the request sinful?

> What did God reveal about the source and pattern of Israel's decision making?

> What connection is made between the treatment of Samuel and the treatment of God?

> How does the implication that a relationship with God is reflected in earthly relationships extend beyond Samuel to all people?

> Why did God give the people what they wanted?

> What else does this text teach us about God? Ourselves?

> What other questions or observations do you have?

NOTE: Provide ample time for group members to share responses and questions about the text. Don't feel pressured to prioritize the printed agenda over group members' personal experiences. If time allows, discuss responses to the questions in the personal reading.

❯ OBEY THE TEXT

RESPOND: Foster an environment of openness and action. Help individuals apply biblical truth to specific areas of personal thought, attitude, and/or behavior.

> How are you tempted to conform to culture instead of being set apart for God's kingdom?

> In what ways do you find yourself looking for security in people or things rather than God?

> How does fear drive decisions rather than faith?

> How are you seeking godly wisdom? How might you be ignoring it?

> Are you primarily surrounded by people who think like you? Who in your life speaks truth even if you don't want to hear it?

> What can you do this week to be set apart and to trust the authority of the King of kings?

PRAY: Close by praying that group members will be set apart from the culture with holy desires and godly character. Ask the Holy Spirit to help each of you trust in God.

❯ GETTING STARTED

OPENING OPTIONS: Choose one of the following to open the group discussion.

WEEKLY QUOTATION DISCUSSION STARTER: "We are half-hearted creatures … far too easily pleased."—C. S. Lewis

A more complete quotation is:

"It would seem that Our Lord finds our desires, not too strong, but too weak. We are half-hearted creatures, fooling about with drink and sex and ambition when infinite joy is offered us, like an ignorant child who wants to go on making mud pies in a slum because he cannot imagine what is meant by the offer of a holiday at the sea. We are far too easily pleased."—C. S. Lewis

> ❯ What's your initial response to this week's quotation?

> ❯ In what ways do you see our culture seeking satisfaction and meaning?

> ❯ How do you see yourself being halfhearted in your devotion to God and in your desire for things of this world?

> ❯ Today we'll see the outcome of halfhearted obedience.

CREATIVE ACTIVITY: Before the group meets, identify a song that easily gets stuck in your head. As the group arrives, play the song while everyone gets settled. If people are familiar with the song, after it's over, clarify that you often find yourself repeating the lyrics or music over and over in your mind or aloud. Then use the following to introduce the point being made.

> ❯ What other songs get stuck in your head? What makes them so catchy? When have you caught yourself humming, singing, or even dancing without realizing it?

> ❯ Today's story will show us how a pattern in someone's heart and mind becomes a pattern of behavior.

❯ UNDERSTAND THE CONTEXT

PROVIDE BACKGROUND: Briefly introduce members to major themes, information, and ideas that will help them understand 1 Samuel 15:7-15,22-23 (see p. 27). Then, to help people personally connect today's context with the original context, use the following questions and statements.

> ❯ What's meant by the popular saying "Partial obedience is disobedience"?

> ❯ When have you experienced or had to lay down consequences for partial obedience?

> ❯ This week we'll see how Saul, the first king of Israel, exhibited a pattern of partial obedience to God.

❯ EXPLORE THE TEXT

READ THE BIBLE: Ask two volunteers to read 1 Samuel 15:7-15,22-23.

DISCUSS: Use the following questions to discuss group members' initial reactions to the text.

> Which people or things did Saul keep? What do Saul's actions reveal about his heart?

> How did God respond to Saul's behavior? What does this response reveal about God's heart?

> What did Samuel feel, do, and say once he was made aware of Saul's sin? Why is the order of Samuel's response significant?

> What justification did Saul make for disobedience? What consequences did he suffer?

> What comparisons did Samuel make in the final verses? What did he contrast? How would you summarize Samuel's final statement?

> What else does this text teach us about God? Ourselves?

> What other questions or observations do you have?

NOTE: Provide ample time for group members to share responses and questions about the text. Don't feel pressured to prioritize the printed agenda over group members' personal experiences. If time allows, discuss responses to the questions in the personal reading.

❯ OBEY THE TEXT

RESPOND: Foster an environment of openness and action. Help individuals apply biblical truth to specific areas of personal thought, attitude, and/or behavior.

> At which of these steps do you struggle to follow Samuel's example of godly confrontation: deep burden, intercessory prayer, speaking directly to the person, and being clear about sin and its consequences? Why are those steps difficult?

> How does God's desire for obedience over religious activity affect your personal relationship with Him? Would you say you're seeking to please Him? Why or why not?

> Partial obedience is equated with idolatry or divination. When you consider areas of personal compromise, partial obedience, or blatant disobedience, what idols are revealed?

> About what do you need accountability? Why are you tempted to compromise in that area of your life? How can we hold you accountable to take steps of obedience?

PRAY: Close by praying that group members will trust God. Confess areas where you struggle with obedience. Ask for courage to hold one another accountable and for humility to be held accountable.

❯ GETTING STARTED

OPENING OPTIONS: Choose one of the following to open the group discussion.

WEEKLY QUOTATION DISCUSSION STARTER: "All that is gold does not glitter."—J. R. R. Tolkien

> ❯ What's your initial response to this week's quotation?

> ❯ When has a person, place, or thing greatly exceeded your expectations? Why were you surprised?

> ❯ Today we'll see the invaluable purpose for someone's life that only God recognized.

CREATIVE ACTIVITY: To prepare, identify the person you consider to be the most popular person in our culture and the person you consider to be the greatest. You may choose to secure pictures of both people. Before the group arrives, specify a few characteristics of each person and of our culture that may contribute to the person's popularity or greatness. After the group has arrived, identify the person you consider to be most popular and use the following questions to start your discussion.

> ❯ What makes this person so popular? Add any of your own opinions after group members provide a few observations.

> ❯ What other person may be most popular in our culture? Why?

> ❯ Whom do you consider to be the greatest person in our culture? Why? Reveal the person you identified as great, along with the reasons you chose him or her.

> ❯ Why are greatness and popularity not necessarily the same thing?

> ❯ Popular expectation and God's choice for greatness aren't the same thing.

❯ UNDERSTAND THE CONTEXT

PROVIDE BACKGROUND: Briefly introduce members to major themes, information, and ideas that will help them understand 1 Samuel 16:4-13 (see p. 37). Then, to help people personally connect today's context with the original context, use the following questions and statements.

> ❯ How do you think Saul would have felt if he had known another king was about to be chosen?

> ❯ If you had been Samuel, what would you have felt after God told you to anoint a new king while Saul was still in power?

> ❯ In today's Scripture passage Samuel will step out in faithful obedience without knowing the outcome of God's direction.

EXPLORE THE TEXT

READ THE BIBLE: Ask a volunteer to read 1 Samuel 16:4-13.

DISCUSS: Use the following questions to discuss group members' initial reactions to the text.

> How does the opening description of Samuel provide insight into his character? How does it reflect God's desire for His chosen king?

> How did each of Samuel's actions relate to his ability to discern God's will?

> Even Samuel made assumptions, but what did God reveal about human wisdom? How is God's declaration about seeing a man's heart convicting? Hopeful?

> What evidence is there that Samuel learned from God's correction?

> After his anointing what happened to David? How is this action related to the Lord's seeing a man's heart? Why is it significant for the future king?

> In what ways does this account foreshadow the coming of Jesus? What else does this text teach us about God? Ourselves?

> What other questions or observations do you have?

NOTE: Provide ample time for group members to share responses and questions about the text. Don't feel pressured to prioritize the printed agenda over group members' personal experiences. If time allows, discuss responses to the questions in the personal reading.

OBEY THE TEXT

RESPOND: Foster an environment of openness and action. Help individuals apply biblical truth to specific areas of personal thought, attitude, and/or behavior.

> Samuel had traveled by faith and then followed God's leading by not choosing the other seven sons. How do you respond to situations in which you can't see the whole plan?

> What are you doing to put yourself in a posture to discern God's will?

> What personal decision are you facing for which you need to trust God's Spirit, instead of popular or personal opinions, to provide direction?

PRAY: Close by praying for the Holy Spirit to work in and through each person's life. Confess any prejudice or assumptions that prevent you from seeing people or circumstances as God sees them. Ask for an awareness of your hearts and for the ability to hear and obey God's will.

❯ GETTING STARTED

OPENING OPTIONS: Choose one of the following to open the group discussion.

WEEKLY QUOTATION DISCUSSION STARTER: "It is curious that physical courage should be so common in the world and moral courage so rare."—Mark Twain

> ❯ What's your initial response to this week's quotation?

> ❯ Whom or what do you think of when you hear the word *courage*? Why?

> ❯ Today we'll see an uncommon courage that boldly chose to do the right thing, regardless of the opponent's overwhelming physical strength.

CREATIVE ACTIVITY: Before the group arrives, identify your favorite inspirational moment from a movie, historical speech, sporting event, story, or quotation. After the group has arrived, start by explaining the context of the words or moment you find inspiring. If possible, find a way to show, play, or read the inspiring moment or words.

> ❯ What's your favorite inspirational speech, quotation, or moment? What makes it inspiring?

> ❯ Why do people love quotations, stories, and speeches like these?

> ❯ Today we'll read the confident words of a true underdog that convinced a king to let him try the impossible.

❯ UNDERSTAND THE CONTEXT

PROVIDE BACKGROUND: Briefly introduce members to major themes, information, and ideas that will help them understand 1 Samuel 17:32-37,42-50 (see p. 47). Then, to help people personally connect today's context with the original context, use the following questions and statements.

> ❯ David was bringing food and supplies to his brothers on the battlefield. He wasn't supposed to be there. Why was this more than a coincidence?

> ❯ When have you been at the right place at the right time for an unexpected opportunity?

> ❯ In the well-known story of David and Goliath, we'll see that God brought David into a situation at just the right time.

❯ EXPLORE THE TEXT

READ THE BIBLE: Ask two volunteers to read 1 Samuel 17:32-37,42-50.

DISCUSS: Use the following questions to discuss group members' initial reactions to the text.

> ❯ How did David identify himself in relationship to King Saul? Why is this significant?

> ❯ How did Saul's initial response to David appear to be wise? How could David's lack of military experience have actually been an advantage?

> ❯ What rationale did David provide for his willingness to enter the deadly conflict? In what ways were his past experiences evidence of God's sovereignty?

> ❯ How did David exemplify faith as both bold and humble?

> ❯ How were David and Goliath's words to each other similar? Why is the difference significant between the way Goliath mentioned his gods and the way David mentioned his God?

> ❯ Although facing Goliath was the specific context, in what way is David's intent a model for all God's people in any context?

> ❯ What else does this text teach us about God? Ourselves?

> ❯ What other questions or observations do you have?

NOTE: Provide ample time for group members to share responses and questions about the text. Don't feel pressured to prioritize the printed agenda over group members' personal experiences. If time allows, discuss responses to the questions in the personal reading.

❯ OBEY THE TEXT

RESPOND: Foster an environment of openness and action. Help individuals apply biblical truth to specific areas of personal thought, attitude, and/or behavior.

> ❯ What difficult or overwhelming situation are you currently facing?

> ❯ As David recalled ways God had proved faithful, who can share a story about God's work in your life?

> ❯ What in your past can you now see as God's sovereign preparation for where you are today, even if that preparation was difficult at the time? In what ways is God's work in your life intended not only to benefit you but also to make Himself known to others through you?

PRAY: Close by praising God for His faithfulness in your lives. Ask for boldness and humility in making Him known to everyone around you. Pray for courage to trust Him no matter what you face.

❯ GETTING STARTED

OPENING OPTIONS: Choose one of the following to open the group discussion.

WEEKLY QUOTATION DISCUSSION STARTER: "I'm not concerned with your liking or disliking me. All I ask is that you respect me as a human being."—Jackie Robinson

> ❯ What's your initial response to this week's quotation?

> ❯ What's the difference between liking and respecting someone?

> ❯ Why would we show respect to someone we don't like?

> ❯ How can Christians respect leaders when we don't like them or even when we have serious disagreements with them?

> ❯ Today we'll see what godly respect looks like for a person in authority.

CREATIVE ACTIVITY: Before the group gathers, look up a current list of U.S. presidents. Starting with the current president, ask who can name the most presidents, going backward in order. If there's a tie, see who can identify each president's political party.

> ❯ On a scale of 1 to 10, with 1 being none and 10 being tremendous, how would you rate your knowledge of local and national leaders?

> ❯ Using the same scale, how would you rate the general level of respect for government leaders in our society? In our religious circles? In your own attitude?

> ❯ Overall, do you think there's social pressure to respect or disrespect people in positions of authority?

> ❯ Today we'll see how David respected the king even when pressured to do otherwise.

❯ UNDERSTAND THE CONTEXT

PROVIDE BACKGROUND: Briefly introduce members to major themes, information, and ideas that will help them understand 1 Samuel 26:7-12,21-25 (see p. 57). Then, to help people personally connect today's context with the original context, use the following questions and statements.

> ❯ After David's humble service to the king and his boldness on behalf of the nation of Israel, why did Saul seek to kill David?

> ❯ What motivates a person's paranoia?

> ❯ This final session climaxes an increasingly tense story emphasizing the theme of faithful integrity in 1 Samuel.

❯ EXPLORE THE TEXT

READ THE BIBLE: Ask two volunteers to read 1 Samuel 26:7-12,21-25.

DISCUSS: Use the following questions to discuss group members' initial reactions to the text.

> ❯ What did Abishai advise David to do? Why would this have seemed to be wise counsel?

> ❯ Why did David refuse to kill an opponent in this situation instead of seizing an opportunity like the one he had against Goliath?

> ❯ In what ways were David's patience and integrity expressions of faith? How did he exercise caution? What details describe God's favor and provision while David was in the camp?

> ❯ How did Saul respond to David's mercy?

> ❯ God would establish a lineage through David that would bring mercy for all sinners through Jesus Christ. What else in this final conversation points us to the gospel?

> ❯ What else does this text teach us about God? Ourselves?

> ❯ What other questions or observations do you have?

NOTE: Provide ample time for group members to share responses and questions about the text. Don't feel pressured to prioritize the printed agenda over group members' personal experiences. If time allows, discuss responses to the questions in the personal reading.

❯ OBEY THE TEXT

RESPOND: Foster an environment of openness and action. Help individuals apply biblical truth to specific areas of personal thought, attitude, and/or behavior.

> ❯ In what way do you currently need to show patience? How can you model faith and integrity while you wait on God's timing?

> ❯ How can you show mercy or respect to someone out of respect for God? How can you honor the godly leaders in our church this week?

> ❯ During this study of 1 Samuel, what has God shown you about leadership? Personal character? Trusting God's will? What application will you take away from studying the lives of Hannah, Samuel, Saul, and David?

PRAY: Close by thanking God for continuing to work in our lives today. Confess any areas of pride and disrespect. Ask God for godly humility in honoring other people, especially those in leadership. Pray for patience and integrity while waiting on God's purposes to be accomplished in His timing.

❯ TIPS FOR LEADING A GROUP

PRAYERFULLY PREPARE

Prepare for each session by—

> **reviewing the weekly material and group questions ahead of time;**

> **praying for each person in the group.**

Ask the Holy Spirit to work through you and the group discussion to help people take steps toward Jesus each week as directed by God's Word.

MINIMIZE DISTRACTIONS

Create a comfortable environment. If group members are uncomfortable, they'll be distracted and therefore not engaged in the group experience. Plan ahead by taking into consideration—

> **seating;**

> **temperature;**

> **lighting;**

> **food or drink;**

> **surrounding noise;**

> **general cleanliness (put pets away if meeting in a home).**

At best, thoughtfulness and hospitality show guests and group members they're welcome and valued in whatever environment you choose to gather. At worst, people may never notice your effort, but they're also not distracted. Do everything in your ability to help people focus on what's most important: connecting with God, with the Bible, and with others.

INCLUDE OTHERS

Your goal is to foster a community in which people are welcome just as they are but encouraged to grow spiritually. Always be aware of opportunities to—

> **invite** new people to join your group;

> **include** any people who visit the group.

An inexpensive way to make first-time guests feel welcome or to invite people to get involved is to give them their own copies of this Bible-study book.

ENCOURAGE DISCUSSION

A good small group has the following characteristics.

> **Everyone participates.** Encourage everyone to ask questions, share responses, or read aloud.

> **No one dominates—not even the leader.** Be sure what you say takes up less than half of your time together as a group. Politely redirect discussion if anyone dominates.

> **Nobody is rushed through questions.** Don't feel that a moment of silence is a bad thing. People often need time to think about their responses to questions they've just heard or to gain courage to share what God is stirring in their hearts.

> **Input is affirmed and followed up.** Make sure you point out something true or helpful in a response. Don't just move on. Build personal connections with follow-up questions, asking how other people have experienced similar things or how a truth has shaped their understanding of God and the Scripture you're studying. People are less likely to speak up if they fear that you don't actually want to hear their answers or that you're looking for only a certain answer.

> **God and His Word are central.** Opinions and experiences can be helpful, but God has given us the truth. Trust Scripture to be the authority and God's Spirit to work in people's lives. You can't change anyone, but God can. Continually point people to the Word and to active steps of faith.

KEEP CONNECTING

Think of ways to connect with members during the week. Participation during the session is always improved when members spend time connecting with one another away from the session. The more people are comfortable with and involved in one another's lives, the more they'll look forward to being together. When people move beyond being friendly and in the same group to truly being friends who form a community, they come to each session eager to engage instead of merely attending.

Encourage group members with thoughts, commitments, or questions from the session by connecting through—

> emails;
> texts;
> social media.

When possible, build deeper friendships by planning or spontaneously inviting group members to join you outside your regularly scheduled group time for—

> meals;
> fun activities;
> projects around your home, church, or community.

❯ GROUP CONTACT INFORMATION

Name _____ Number _____
Email/social media _____

Name _____ Number _____
Email/social media _____

Name _____ Number _____
Email/social media _____

Name _____ Number _____
Email/social media _____

Name _____ Number _____
Email/social media _____

Name _____ Number _____
Email/social media _____

Name _____ Number _____
Email/social media _____

Name _____ Number _____
Email/social media _____

Name _____ Number _____
Email/social media _____

Name _____ Number _____
Email/social media _____

Name _____ Number _____
Email/social media _____